THE PIANO SONGBOOK: CLASSIC SONGS

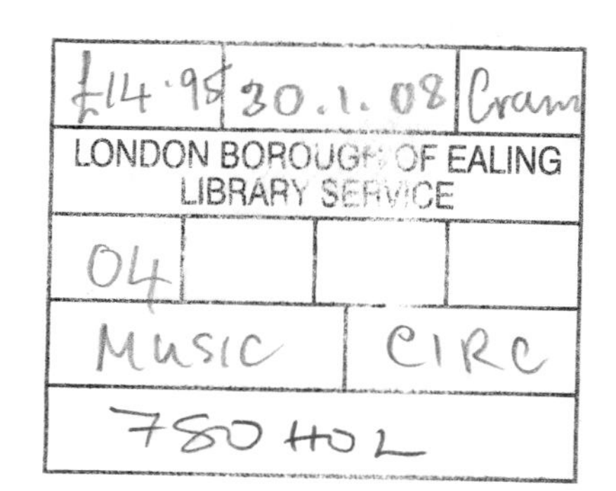

First published by Faber Music Ltd in 2007
3 Queen Square, London WC1N 3AU

Arranged by Camden Music & Lucy Holliday
Engraved by Camden Music
Compiled & edited by Lucy Holliday

Designed by Lydia Merrills-Ashcroft
Photograph from Redferns Music Picture Library

Printed in England by Caligraving Ltd

The text paper used in this publication is a virgin fibre product
that is manufactured in the UK to ISO 14001 standards.
The wood fibre used is only sourced from managed forests using
sustainable forestry principles. This paper is 100% recyclable

ISBN10: 0-571-52899-6
EAN13: 978-0-571-52899-8

To buy Faber Music publications or to find out
about the full range of titles available,
please contact your local music retailer
or Faber Music sales enquiries:

Faber Music Ltd, Burnt Mill, Elizabeth Way,
Harlow, CM20 2HX England
Tel: +44(0)1279 82 89 82 Fax: +44(0)1279 82 89 83
sales@fabermusic.com fabermusic.com

THE PIANO SONGBOOK: CLASSIC SONGS

BECAUSE THE NIGHT

Words and Music by Bruce Springsteen and Patti Smith

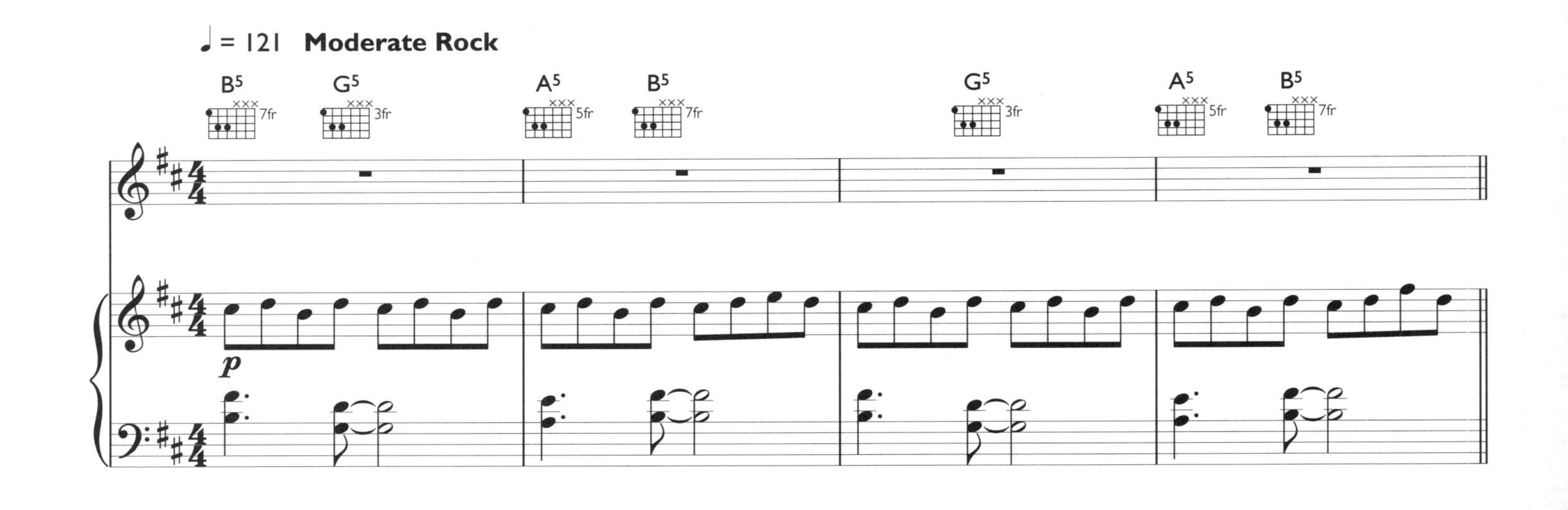

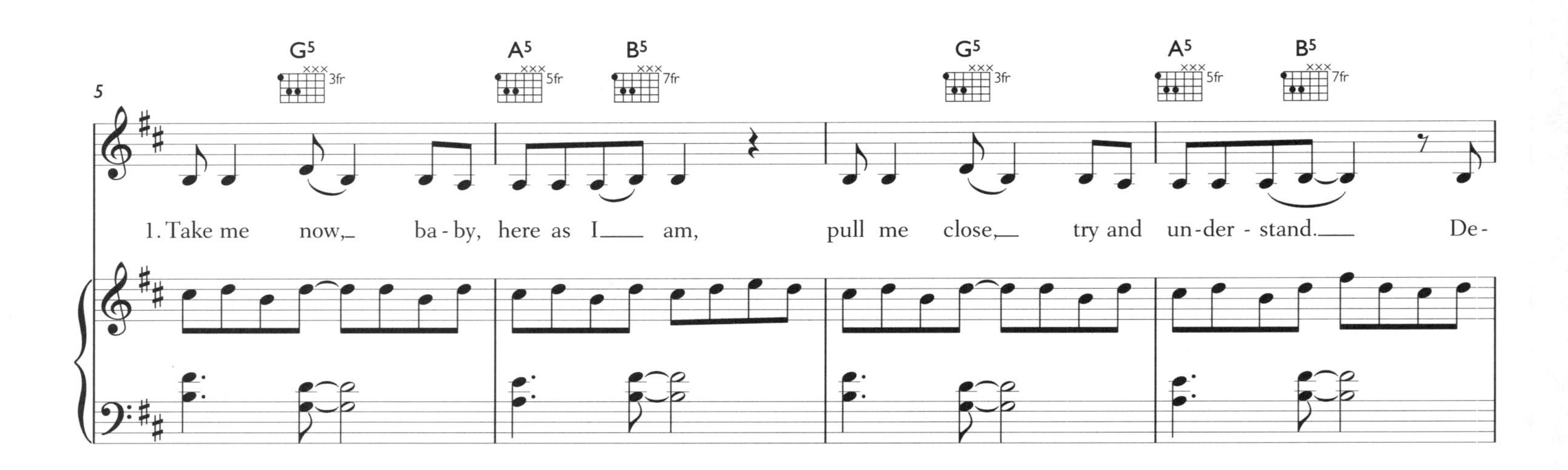

Heavier
Gmaj7
A
D
A
Bm
Gmaj7
G(add2)
Gmaj7
A
13
Come on now, try and un - der - stand the way I feel when I'm in your hands,
mf
D
Gmaj7
G(add2)
Gmaj7
A
C
Bm
17
take my hand, come un - der - co - ver, they can't hurt you now, can't hurt you now,
F♯sus4
F♯
Bm
Em/G
G
A
21
can't hurt you now.
Be - cause the night be - longs to lov - ers,
f heavily accented
Bm
Em/G
G
A
Bm
Em/G
G
A
25
be - cause the night be - longs to lust, be - cause the night be - longs to lov - ers,

29
Bm Em/G G A Bm B5 G5 A5 B5
7fr 3fr 5fr 7fr
be-cause the night be-longs to us. 2. Have I doubt when I'm a-lone?
mp
Bass Gtr.
33
G5 A5 B5 G5 A5 B5
Love is a ring, the te-le-phone. Love is an an-gel dis-guised as lust,
37
G5 A5 B5 Gmaj7 A D A
here in our bed un-til the mor-ning comes. Come on now, try and un-der-stand the
mf
41
Bm Gmaj7 G(add2) Gmaj7 A D Gmaj7 G(add2) Gmaj7 A
way I feel un-der your com-mand. Take my hand as the sun des-cends, they

C
Bm
F♯sus4
F♯
45
can't touch you now,
can't touch you now,
can't touch you now.
Bm
Em/G
G
A
49
Be-cause the night be-longs to lov-ers,
be-cause the night be-longs to lust
f heavily accented
53
Be-cause the night be-longs to lov-ers,
be-cause the night be-longs to us.
Gmaj7
A
D
57
Guitar Solo

D
Gmaj7
A
Gsus2
61
With
fp
65
love we sleep, with doubt the vi-cious cir-cle turns and burns with-out you I can-not
Bm
mf
sim.
69
live, for-give, the yearn - ing, burn-ing, I be-lieve it's time, too real to feel, so
G
73
touch me now, touch me now, touch me now.
F♯

77
Bm Em/G G A Bm Em/G G A Bm
Be-cause the night be-longs to lov-ers, be-cause the night be-longs to lust.
f
81
Em/G G A Bm Em/G G A Bm
Be-cause the night be-longs to lov-ers, be-cause the night be-longs to us.
85
Bm Em/G G A Bm Em/G G A Bm
Be-cause to-night there are two lov-ers, if we be-lieve in the night we trust.
89
Em/G G A Bm Em/G G A Bm
Repeat to fade
Be-cause the night be-longs to lov-ers, be-cause the night be-longs to love.

EMBARRASMENT

Words and Music by Michael Barson and Lee Thompson

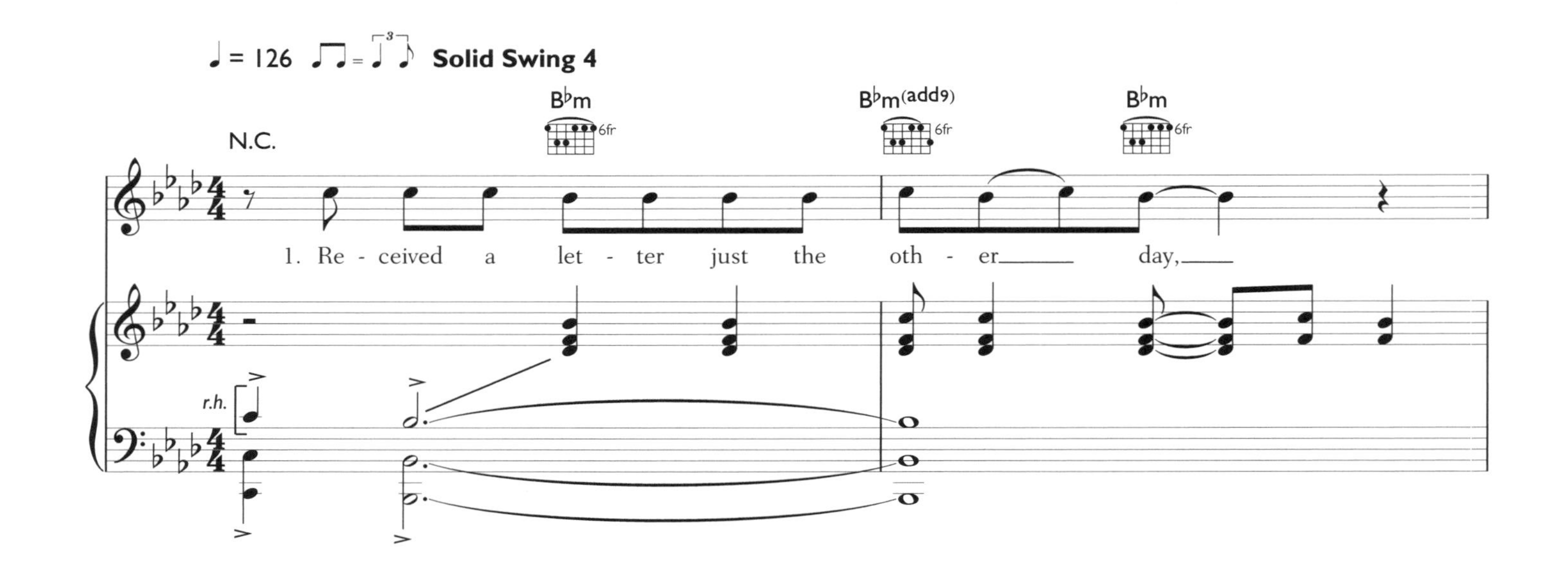

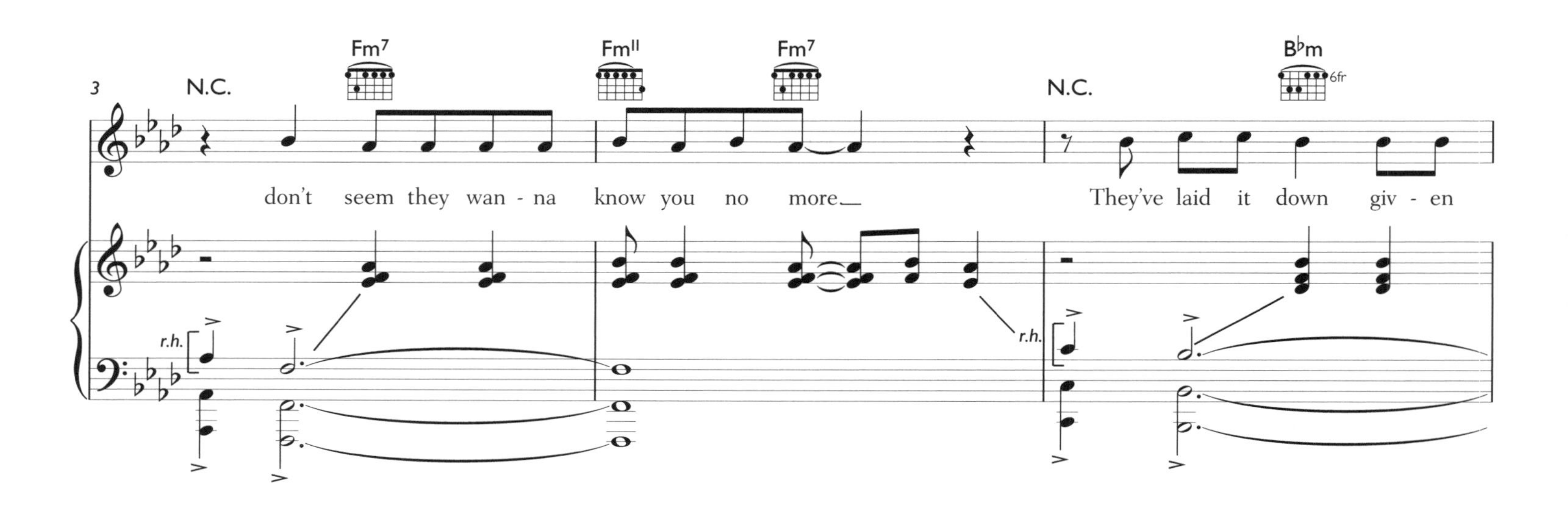

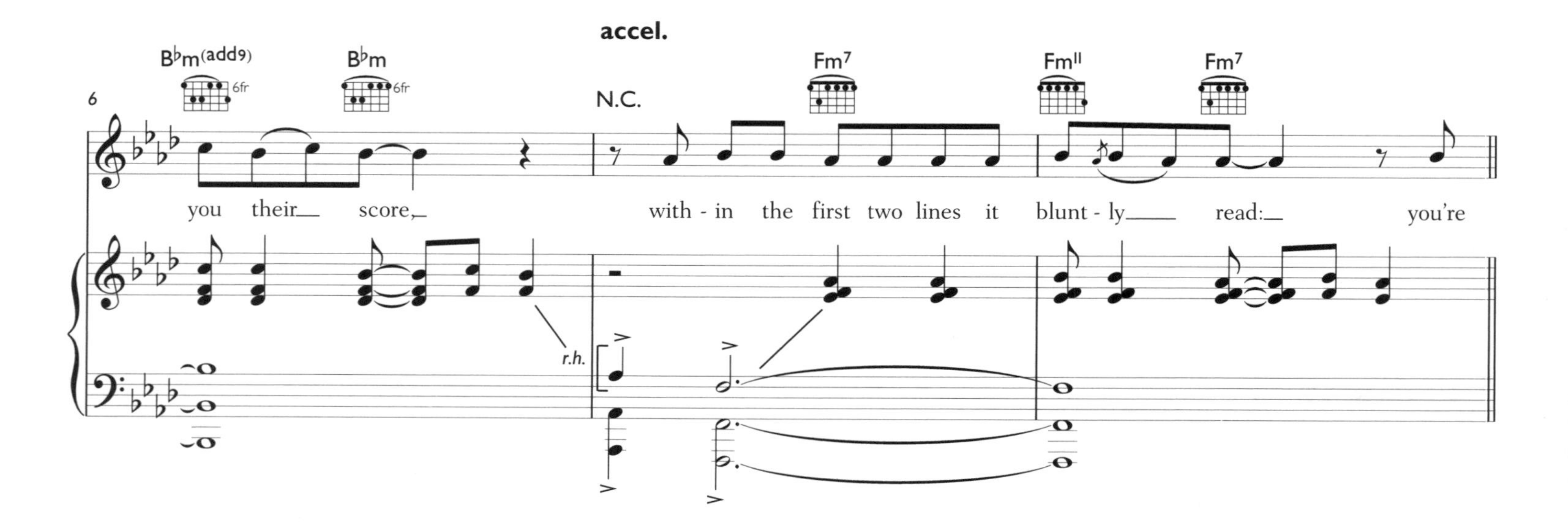

♩ = 144 with a moderate beat
E♭6 E♭ E♭6 E♭ Gm11 Gm7 Gm11 Gm7
not to come see us no more, keep a-way from our door,
stacc. sim.
B♭m(add9) B♭m B♭m(add9) B♭m Cm7 Fm7 Cm7 Fm7
don't come 'round here no more, what on earth did you do that for?
E♭6 E♭ E♭6 E♭ Gm11 Gm7 Gm11 Gm7
Our Aunt, she don't wan-na know she says, what will the neigh-bours think? They'll think,
B♭m(add9) B♭m B♭m(add9) B♭m Cm7 Fm7 Cm7 Fm7
we don't, that's what they'll think, we don't, but I will, 'cause I know they think I don't.

D♭6
D♭
D♭6
D♭
4fr
Fm11
Fm7
Fm11
Fm7
25
3
Our Un-cle he don't wan-na_ know,_ he says we are a dis-grace to the hum-an_ race,_ he says,
A♭add9
A♭
A♭add9
A♭
4fr
D♭/E♭
E♭
29
3
how can you show your_ face_ when you're a dis-grace to the hu-man race?_
B♭m(add9)
B♭m
B♭m(add9)
B♭m
6fr
Fm11
Fm7
Fm11
Fm7
33
Sax solo
B♭m(add9)
B♭m
B♭m(add9)
B♭m
6fr
Fm11
Fm7
Fm11
Fm7
37

N.C. B♭m B♭m(add9) B♭m N.C. Fm7 Fm11 Fm7
2. They've made a com-mit-ment, you're an em-bar-rass-ment, yes, an em-bar-rass-ment, a liv-ing en-dorse-ment.
N.C. B♭m B♭m(add9) B♭m N.C. Fm7 Fm11 Fm7
The in-ten-tion that you have booked was an in-ten-tion that was o-ver-looked.
E♭6 E♭ E♭6 E♭ Gm11 Gm7 Gm11 Gm7
They say, stay a-way, don't want you home to-day,
B♭m(add9) B♭m B♭m(add9) B♭m Cm7 Fm7 Cm7 Fm7
keep a-way from our door, don't come a-round here no more
r.h.

E♭6
E♭
Gm11
Gm7
Our Dad, don't wan-na know, he says, this is a se-ri-ous mat-ter,
B♭m(add9)
B♭m
Cm7
Fm7
too late to re-con-si-der, no one's gon-na wan-na know ya!
D♭6
D♭
Fm11
Fm7
Our Mum, she don't wan-na know, she says, I'm feel-ing twice as old, she says,
A♭add9
A♭
D♭/E♭
thought she had her head on her shoul-ders, 'cause I'm feel-ing twice as old-er,

E♭/F
F
Cm(add9)
Cm
73
I'm feel - ing twice as old - er.
Sax solo ad lib.
Gm11
Gm7
77
81
1.2.
3.
Slightly slower
84
N.C.
You're an em - bar - rass - ment…
Organ
r.h.
8fr
3fr

EVERYBODY'S GOT TO LEARN SOMETIME

Words and Music by James Warren

D♯m7♭5
G♯m
4fr
A
16
ev - 'ry - bo - dy's got - ta learn some - time,
mm,
19
7fr
ev - 'ry - bo - dy's got - ta learn some - time,
mm, mm.
E
E(♭5)
C♯m7
21
2. Change your heart,
A♯m7♭5
A6
24
look a - round you.
Change your heart,
3

A#m7b5
A6
C#m7
28
it will a-stound you.
I need your lov-in',
G#aug
G#7
F#add9
F#add9/B
B9
32
mm, like the sun - shine.
And
G#m
A
D#m7b5
35
ev'ry-bo-dy's got-ta learn some-time,
ev'-ry-bo-dy's got-ta learn some-time,
38
mm,
ev'-ry-bo-dy's got-ta learn some-time,
mm, mm.

41
E
E(b5)
7fr
G#m
4fr
A
Ev-'ry-bo-dy's got-ta learn some-time,
44
D#m7b5
oh,
ev-'ry-bo-dy's got-ta learn some-time,
mm,
47
ev-'ry-bo-dy's got-ta learn some-time,
some-time.
49

EVERYBODY HURTS

Words and Music by William Berry, Michael Stipe,
Peter Buck and Michael Mills

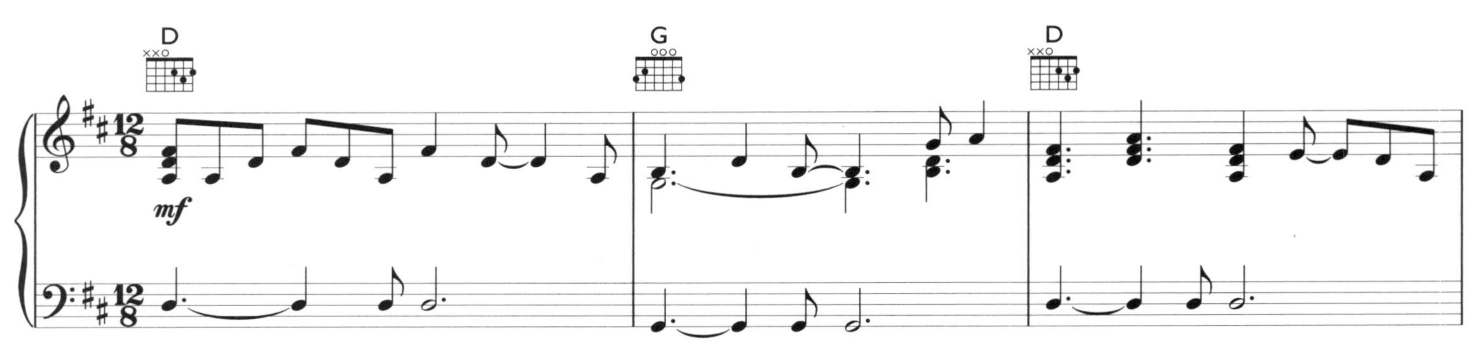

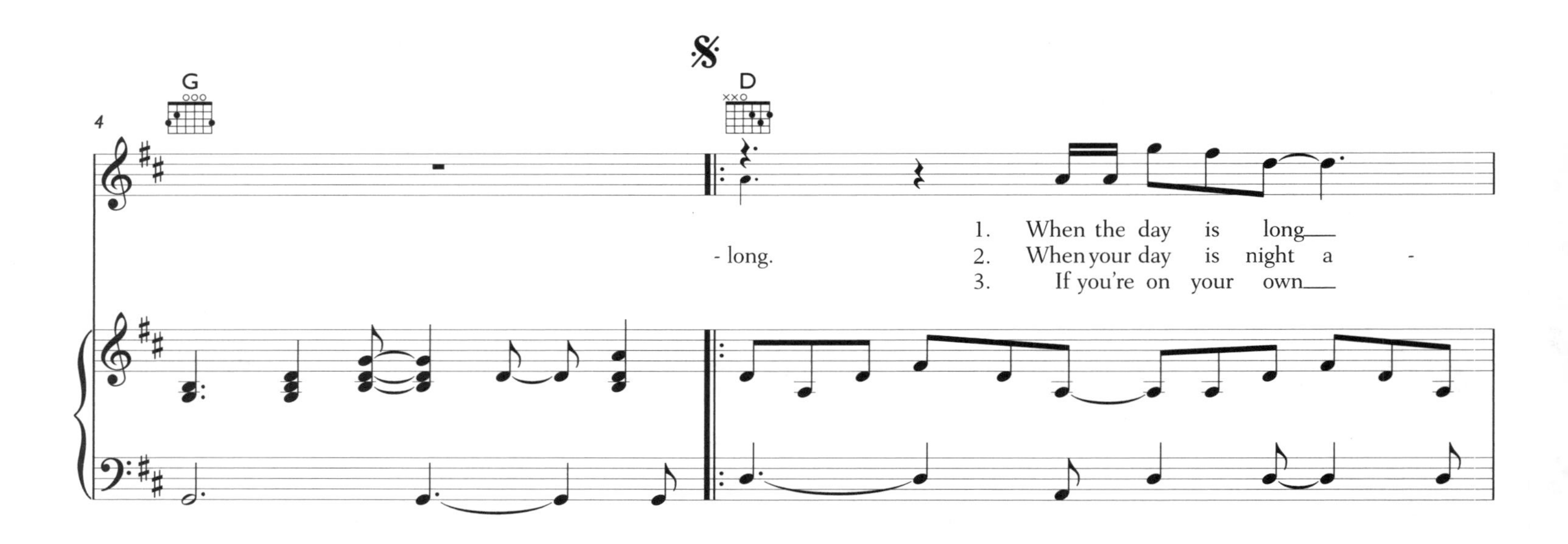

G
D
when you're sure you've had e-
when you think you've had too
when you think you've had too
G
D
-nough of this life, well, hang on.
much of this life, well, hang on.
much of this life to hang on.
G
Em
A
Don't let your-self go,
'Cause ev-'ry-bo-dy hurts,
Well, ev-'ry-bo-dy hurts some-
Em
A
ev-'ry-bo-dy cries
take com-fort in your friends.
-times, ev-'ry-bo-dy cries.

Em
To Coda
1.
A
N.C
and ev - 'ry - bo - dy hurts some -
Ev - 'ry - bo - dy
And ev - 'ry - bo - dy
D
G
- times
Some - times ev - 'ry - thing is
wrong.
Now it's time to sing a -
2.
F#7
hurts.
Don't throw your hand.

Bm
F♯7
Bm
25
Oh,
no.
F♯7
Bm
28
Don't throw
your hand.
C
G
30
If you feel like
you're a - lone,
C
G/B
Am
N.C.
D.𝄋 al Coda
32
no,
no,
no,
you are not a - lone

Coda
A
N.C.
D
hurts some - - times
G
D
G
And ev - 'ry - bo - dy hurts some - times. So, hold
D7
G7
on, hold on. Hold
D7
G7
repeat to fade
on, hold on. Hold

HALLELUJAH, I LOVE HER SO

Words and Music by Ray Charles

E♭7 E7 F7 B♭ N.C. B♭/D N.C. B♭9
loves me so. Ev - 'ry morn - in' 'fore the sun comes up,
E♭ N.C. Edim7 N.C. B♭/F D7/F♯
she brings my cof - fee in my fav - 'rite cup. That's why I know, whoa, I
Gm E♭7 C7 F7sus4 B♭ E♭7 E7 F7
know, I, hal - le - lu - jah I just love her so.
B♭7 E♭7 E7 F7 B♭7
2. When I'm in trou - ble and I have no friends, I know she'll go with me un -
(Tenor Sax. solo on D.𝄋)

E♭7 E7 F7 B♭ N.C. B♭/D N.C. B♭9
-til the end. Ev-'ry-bo-dy asks me how I know,
E♭ N.C. Edim7 N.C. B♭/F D7/F♯
I smile at them and say she told me so. That's why I know, whoa, I
Gm E♭7 C7 F7sus4 B♭ E13 E♭7
know, hal-le-lu-jah I just love her so.
N.C. Edim7 N.C. Edim7 B♭/F N.C.
Now if I call her on the te-le-phone, and tell her that I'm
(Vocal return on D. 𝄋)

37
B♭
N.C.
E13
E♭9
5fr
N.C.
all a - lone,
by the time I count from
39
D♭6
4fr
N.C.
D♭6
4fr
C7
3fr
N.C.
one to four,
I hear her
on my door,
yeah.
(knock)
42
B♭7
6fr
E♭7
6fr
E7
7fr
F7
8fr
B♭7
6fr
In the eve - ning when the
sun goes down,
when there is no - bo - dy
45
E♭7
6fr
E7
7fr
F7
8fr
B♭
6fr
N.C.
B♭/D
N.C.
B♭9
else a - round,
she kiss - es me and she
holds me tight,

48
E♭ 6fr
N.C.
Edim7 6fr
N.C.
B♭/F
D7/F♯
and tells me, "Ray Charles, ev - 'ry - thing's al - right." That's why I know, yes I
51
To Coda
1.
2.
D.% al Coda
Gm 3fr
E♭7 6fr
C7 3fr
F7sus4
B♭
E♭7 6fr
E7 7fr
F7 8fr
E♭7 6fr
E7 7fr
F7 8fr
know, hal - le - lu - jah I just love her so.
Coda
55
B♭
G7
C7
F7sus4
B♭
G7
Yeah, hal - le - lu - jah I just love her so. Yeah, hal - le -
58
C7
F7sus4
B♭
E♭7 6fr
E7 7fr
F7 8fr
B♭7 6fr
- lu - jah I just love her so.

I FEEL THE EARTH MOVE

Words and Music by Carole King

E♭maj7
A♭maj7
Fm7
B♭11
6fr
13
- by, when I see your face, mel - low as the month of May, oh, dar -
- ling, when you're near me, and you ten - der - ly call my name, I know
To Coda
E♭maj7
Fm
Gm
A♭maj7
Fm7
B♭11
G11
3fr
6fr
5fr
17
- ling, I can't stand it when you look at me that way. I feel the
that my e - mo - tions are some - thing I just can't tame,
2.
Cm9
F6/C
Cm7
F6/C
3fr
21
you're a - round
Cm7
F/C
Cm7
F7
3fr
3fr
8fr
25

Cm7
F/C
F7
CmII
3fr
D.% al Coda
BbII
Ooh, dar -
Coda
GII
5fr
I just got to have you ba - by.
Ah, ah, ah,
ah, ah, ah, yeah.

F/C
Cm7
3fr
I feel the earth move un-der my feet, I feel the sky tum-bl-in' down, a-
-tum-bl-in' down, I feel the earth move un - der my feet, I feel the sky tum-bl-in' down, a-
-tum-bl-in' down. I just-a lose con-trol, down to my ve - ry soul
F7
I get all hot and cold all o - ver, all o - ver, all o -
mp

61
F6/C
Cm7
3fr
-ver, all o-ver. I feel the earth move under my feet, I feel the sky tum-bl-in' down, a-
f
65
F6/C
Cm7
F6/C
Cm7
-tum-bl-in' down, I feel the earth move under my feet, I feel the sky tum-bl-in' down, a-
rall.
69
F6/C
Cm7
B♭/C
-tum-bl-in' down, a-tum-bl-in' down, a-tum-bl-in' down, a-tum-bl-in' down,
72
A♭maj7/C
B♭/C
tum-bl-in' down.
mp

I'LL STAND BY YOU

Words and Music by Chrissie Hynde,
Tom Kelly and Billy Steinberg

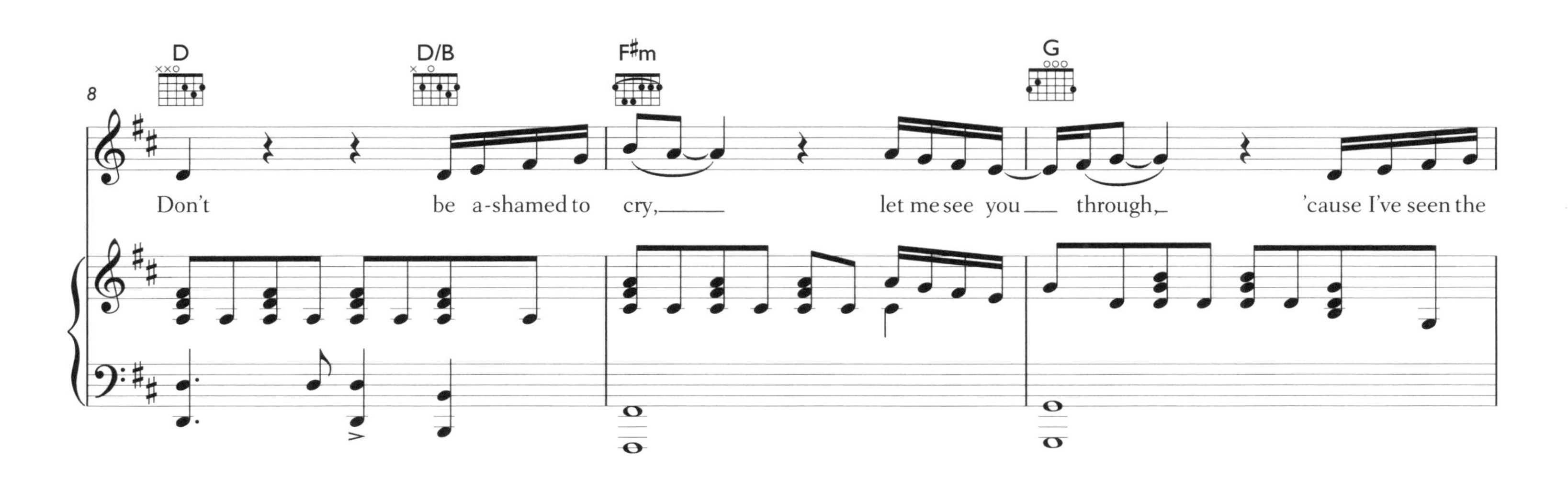

Bm
A
F#m11
Bm
F#m11
Bm
11
dark side too_ When the night_ falls on you, you don't know_ what to do, no-thing you con-
G
A
D
14
- fess,___ could make me love you__ less. I'll stand by you, I'll stand by_
Bm
Am7
G
D
F
G
3fr
17
__ you._ Won't let no-bo-dy hurt__ you,___ I'll stand by you.
C
Em
F
20
2. So, if you're mad,__ get mad,_ don't hold it all in - side, come on and talk to

C/G G/B C Em
23
me now. Hey, what you got to hide? I get an-gry
F Am G Em Am
26
too, well I'm a lot like you. When you're stand-ing at the cross-roads, and don't
Em Am F Csus2/G
29
know which path to choose, let me come a-long, 'cause ev-en if you're wrong, I'll stand by
D Bm Am7 G
32
you, I'll stand by you. Won't let no-bo-dy hurt you, I'll stand by

D
Bm7
35
you. Take me in in-to your dark-est hour, and I'll nev-er des-ert
Am7
D
Bm7
37
you, I'll stand by you.
G
Bm
A
F♯m11
Bm
40
And when, when the night falls
F♯m11
Bm
G
A
A/C♯
44
on you ba-by, you're feel-ing all a-lone, you won't be on your own. I'll stand by

D
Bm7
Am7
G
47
you, I'll stand by you, won't let no-bo-dy hurt you, I'll stand by
50
you. Take me in in-to your dark-est hour and I'll nev-er des-ert you, I'll stand by
53
you, I'll stand by you, won't let no-bo-dy hurt you, I'll stand by
56
Repeat to fade
you. Won't let no-bo-dy hurt you, I'll stand by

I LOVE L.A.

Words and Music by Randy Newman

♩ = 130
D
F♯m
C♯m
E
D
F♯m
C♯m
E
A
D
A
E7
Roll - in' down th'Im - per - ial High - way, with a big nas - ty
A
D
F♯m
A
red-head at my side; San - ta A - na wind blow - in' hot from the north, we was

23
F♯m
E7
A
E7
born to ride.
Roll down the win-dow,
26
A
D
F♯m
A
3
put down the top,
crank up the Beach Boys, ba-by,
don't let the mu - sic stop,
29
E7
F♯m
we're gon-na ride it till we
just can't ride it no more.
32
D
F♯m
C♯m
4fr
From the South Bay to the Val - ley,

35
E
D
F♯m
from the West Side to the East Side, ev-'ry-bo-dy's
38
C♯m
4fr
E
ve-ry hap-py, 'cause the sun is shi-ning all the time: looks like a-
3
41
(G)
A
F♯m
-noth-er per-fect day. I love L. A.
44
E7
A
F♯m
E7
A
(We love it!) I love

F♯m
E7
A
F♯m
E7
L. A.
(We love it!)
We love it!
Slightly slower, plodding
F
Am
B♭
Fmaj7
Fm
E♭
Tempo I ♩ = 130
G
Backing vocals
Ah,
ah,
ah,
ah.
G9
C
G7
Look at that moun-tain,

62
C
F
Am
C
look at those trees,
look at that bum o - ver there, man, he's down on his knees;
65
G7
Am
F
look at these wom - en:
ain't no - thin' like 'em no - where.
68
Am
F
Am
Cen - t'ry Boul - e - vard,
(we love it),
71
F
Am
Vic - t'ry Boul - e - vard,
(we love it),
San - ta Mon - i - ca Boul - e - vard,

F
G
G7
G9
74
(we love it), Sixth Street, (we love it, we love it, we love it!)
C
A♭/C
B♭/C
G/C
3fr
78
We love_ L. A.!
Instrumental
82
3
86

90
C
A♭/C
B♭/C
G/C
3fr
94
C
Am
G7
C
Am
I love L. A.
(We love it!)
2° only
Oo, oo. Oo,
98
G7
C
Am
G7
C
I love L. A.
(We love it!)
oo. Oo, oo.

KARMA POLICE

Words and Music by Thomas Yorke, Jonathan Greenwood,
Philip Selway, Colin Greenwood and Edward O'Brien

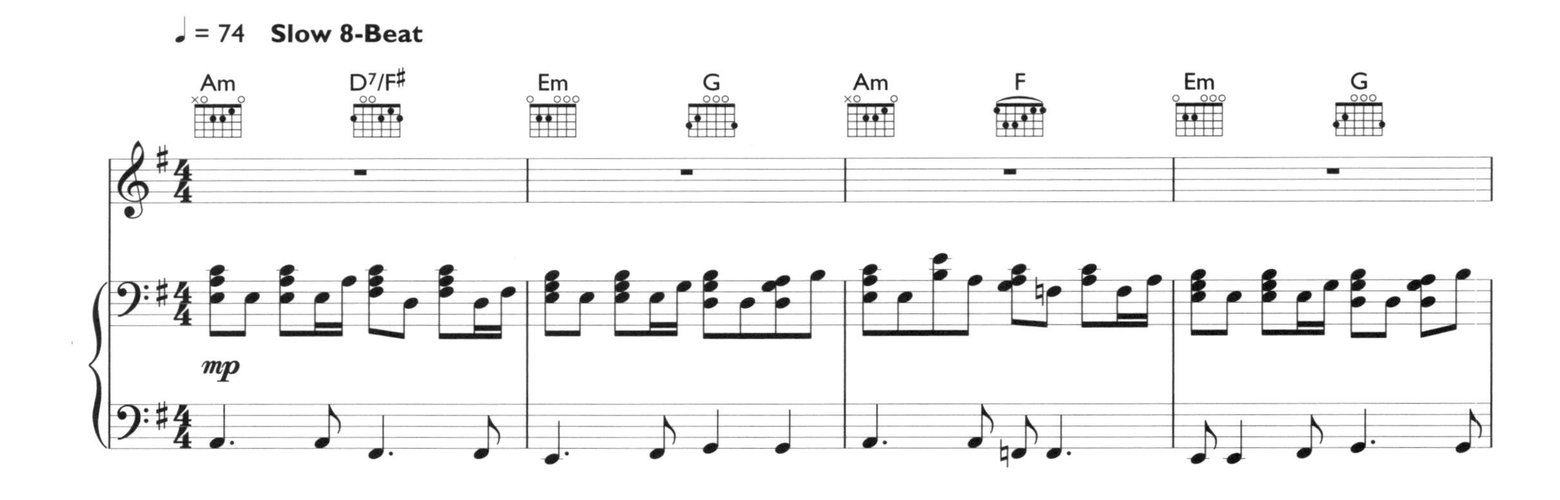

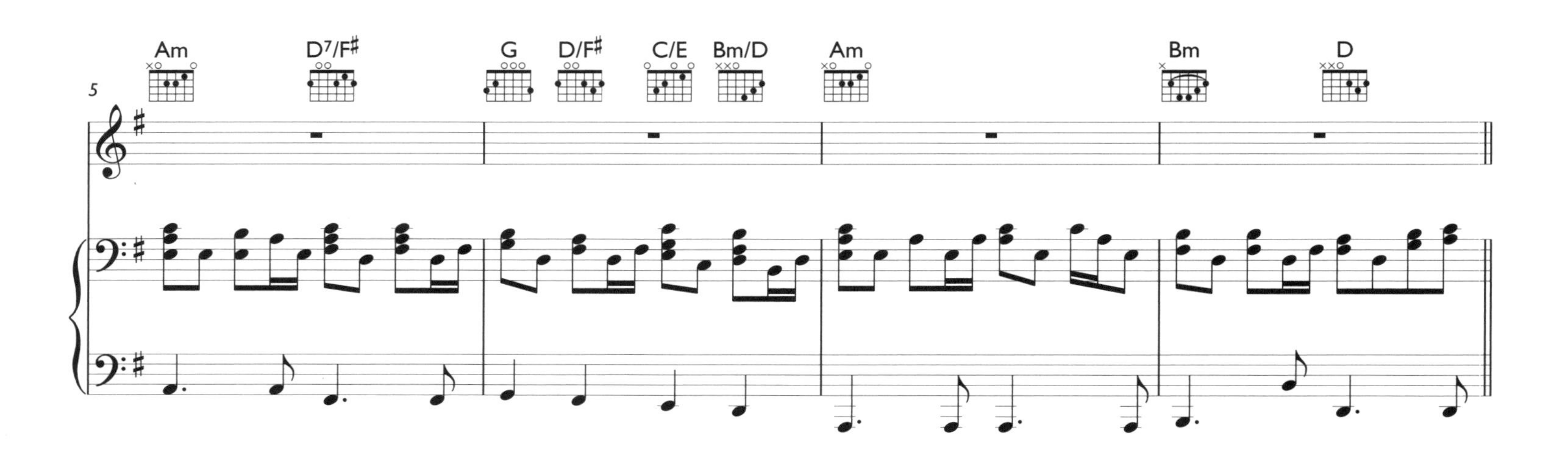

Am D G D/F♯ C/E Bm/D Am Bm D Dsus4 D
13
he's like a de - tuned ra - di - o.
Am D7/F♯ Em G Am F Em G
17
Kar - ma po - lice, ar - rest this girl, her Hit - ler hair - do is mak - ing me feel ill,
Am D G D/F♯ C/E Bm/D Am Bm D
21
and we have crashed her par - ty.
C D G F♯7 4fr C D G F♯7 4fr
25
This is what you get, this is what you get,

C
D
Dsus4
D
G
Bm
C
this is what you get when you mess with us.
Bm
D
Dsus4
D
Am
D7/F#
Em
G
Kar - ma po - lice,
I've giv - en all I can,
Am
F
Em
G
Am
D
it's not e - nough,
I've giv - en all I can,
but we're still on
G
D/F#
C/E
Bm/D
Am
Bm
D
Dsus4
D
the pay - roll.

C D G F#7 C D G F#7
This is what you get,
this is what you get,
C D G Bm C
this is what you get when you mess with us.
Bm/F# Bm Dadd9 G D
For a minute there, I lost myself,
G D Eadd9 E Bm Dadd9
I lost myself.
Phew, for a minute there,

G D G D Eadd9 E
54
I lost my - self, I lost my - self.
Bm D G D G D
57
Ah... ah... ah...
optional bass
Esus4 E Bm Dadd9 G D
60
Oh, for a min - ute there, I lost my - self,
G D Eadd9 E Bm Dadd9
63
I lost my - self. Phew, for a min - ute there,

G
D
Eadd9
E
I lost my - self,
I lost my - self.
Bm
Dadd9
2fr
10fr
Synth.
N.C.

LABELLED WITH LOVE

Words by Chris Difford
Music by Glenn Tilbrook

E
smells like the cat, and the neigh-bours she sick-ens. The black and white T. V. has
learned from a dis tance how love was a les-son. He be-came drink-er and
E7
A
long seen a pic - ture, the cross on the wall is a per - ma-nent fix - ture. The
she be-came moth - er, she knew that one day she'd be one or the oth - er. He
B7
post - man de-liv-ers the fi - nal re-min-ders, she sells off her sil - ver and
ate him-self old-er, drunk him-self diz - zy; proud of her fea - tures, she
A
E/G#
F#m
E
poo - dles in Chi - na.
kept her - self pret - ty.

E
F♯m
B
Drinks to re - mem - ber I, me and my - self, and winds up the clock and knocks
mf
E
F♯m7
dust from the shelf. Home is a love that I miss ve - ry much, so the
B
To Coda
A
E/G♯
F♯m
E
1.
past has been bot - tled and la - belled with love.
2.
E
E
love.
3. He, like a cow - boy, died drunk in his slum - ber,

B7
out on the porch in the mid-dle of sum - mer. She crossed the o - cean back
E
home to her fam - ily, but they had re - ti - red to roads that were san - dy. She
E9
moved home a - lone with-out friends or re - la - tions; lived in a world full of age
A
B7
res - er - va - tion. On moth - eat - en arm - chairs she'd say that she'd sod all, the

A
E/G♯
F♯m
E
D.𝄋 al Coda
friends who had left her to drink from the bot - tle.
⊕ Coda
la - belled with love.
Drinks to re - mem - ber I,
mf
F♯m
B
me and my - self, winds up the clock and knocks dust from the shelf.
F♯m7
Home is a love that I miss ve - ry much, so the past has been bot - tled and

rit.
A E/G♯ F♯m E B7 A E/G♯ F♯m E
61
la - belled with love. The past has been bot - tled and la - belled with love. The

B A G♯m F♯m
4fr
64
past has been bot - tled, and la - belled with

a tempo
E
Repeat to fade
67
love.

MY BABY JUST CARES FOR ME

Words by Gus Kahn
Music by Walter Donaldson

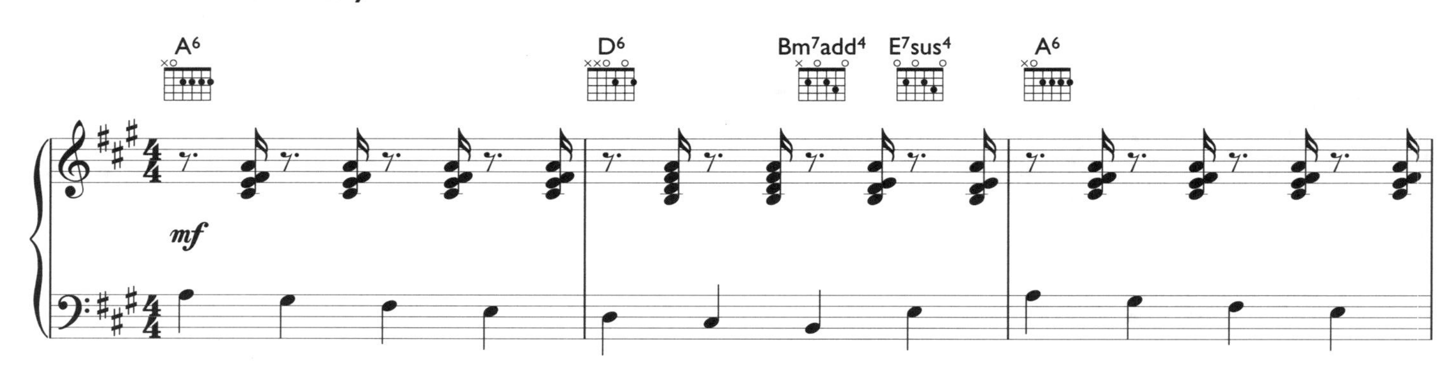

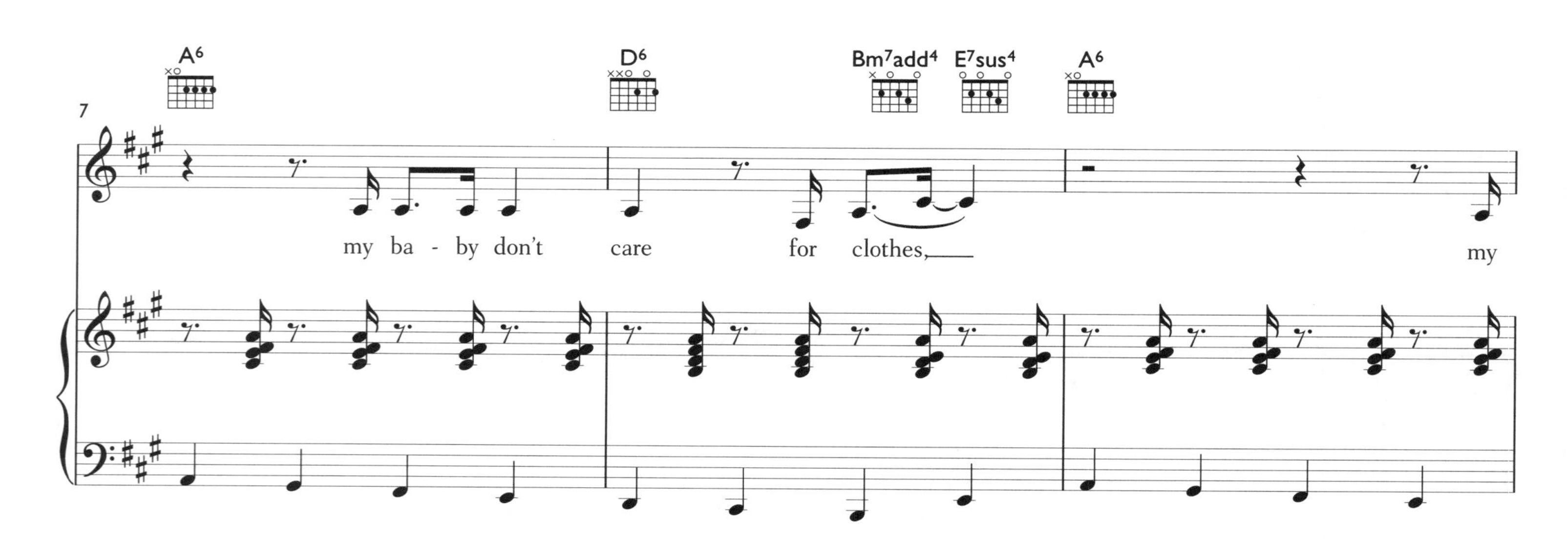

10
Bm7
E11
ba - by just cares for me.
13
C♯m7/11
C♯7
F♯m7
4fr
4fr
2fr
3
My ba - by don't care for cars
16
B9
and ra - ces, my ba - by don't care for
3
19
E11
N.C.
A6
high toned pla - ces. Liz Tay - lor is

D6
Bm7add4
E7sus4
A6
22
not his style
and ev - en La - na Tur - ner's smile,
25
some - thing he can't see.
28
G#7
4fr
My ba - by don't care
A7/G
F#7
Bm7
31
who knows it,
my ba - by just cares

E7
A6
D6
Bm7add4
E7
34
for me.
A6
D6
Bm7add4
E7sus4
A6
37
D6
Bm7add4
E7sus4
A
40
p
Bm7
E11
C♯7
4fr
43
mp
F♯m
46

49
B7
E7
N.C.
52
E7
A6
D6
Bm7add4
E7sus4
subito f
mf
55
A6
D6
Bm7add4
E7sus4
A
mf
58
D6

D
G♯7
4fr
A
Em/G
61
cresc.
F♯7
Bm7
64
E11
E7
E7sus4
A
F♯m7
66
ff
Bm7
E11
E7
A6
D6
Bm7add4
E7sus4
68
Ba - by,
my ba - by don't care for
mp

A6
D6
Bm7add4
E7sus4
A6
71
shows_ and he don't ev - en care for clothes,
Bm7
E7
74
he cares_ for me_
C♯7
4fr
F♯m7
77
My ba - by don't care_ for cars_
B9
80
_ and_ ra - ces, ba - - - - by don't care_ for,

E13sus4
N.C.
A6
83
he don't care for high toned pla - ces. Liz Tay - lor is
mf
D6
Bm7add4
E7sus4
A6
D6
E7
86
not his style and ev - en Li - be - ra - ce's smiles
A6
A7/C#
D6
89
some - thing he can't see.
92
G#7
4fr
Is some - thing he can't see, I won - der what's wrong

A6
Em/G
F#7
Bm7
95
with ba - - - by.
My ba - by just cares
E6
E7
A/C#
Em6
98
for,
my ba - by just
cresc.
F#7
Bm7
E6
E7
100
cares for,
my ba - by just cares
for
103
N.C.
A6
me.
f

PIANO MAN

Words and Music by Billy Joel

F/A
C/G
F
C/E
D
25
Sat - ur - day,
the reg - u - lar crowd shuf - fles in,
G
C
G/B
Fadd9/A
C/G
30
there's an old man
sit - ting next to me
mak - in'
Fadd9/A
G9sus4
C
G/B
35
love to his ton - ic and gin.
F/A
C/G
F
F/G
C
41
cresc.

F/C C G/B F/A C/G
He says, "Son, can you play me a memory? I'm
wait-ress is prac-tis-ing pol-i-tics as the bus-
F C/E D G C G/B
not real-ly sure how it goes, but it's sad and it's sweet and I
-'ness-men slow-ly get stoned. Yes they're shar-ing a drink they call
To Coda I
F/A C/G F F/G C G/B
knew it com-plete when I wore a young-er man's clothes."
lone-li-ness, but it's bet-ter than drink-in' a-
Am Am/G D/F♯ F Am
La, la, la, li, di, da. La, la,

Am/G
D/F♯
D
G
G/F
C/E
G⁷/D
70
li, di, da, da, dum.
cresc.
C
G/B
F/A
C/G
F
C/E
77
Sing us a song, you're the pia - no man,
sing us a song to - night.
f
8vb
D
G
C
G/B
Fadd9/A
C/G
83
Well, we're all in the mood for a mel - o - dy and
Fadd9
F/G
C
G/B
89
you've got us feel - in' al - right.
mf

95
Fadd9/A C/G F F/G C F/C
8vb
101
Cmaj7 F/C C Dm7/C C F/C Cmaj7
106
F/C C Dm/C C G/B F/A C/G
Now John at the bar is a friend of mine, he
It's a pret-ty good crowd for a Sat-ur-day and the
mf
111
F C/E D G C
gets me my drinks for free. And he's quick with a joke
man-a-ger gives me a smile 'cause he knows that it's

To Coda II
G/B
F/A
C/G
Fadd9
G9sus
or to light up your smoke, but there's some-place that he'd rath - er be.
me they've been com - ing to see to for - get a - bout life for a while.
C
F/C
D.% al Coda I
And the
cresc.
Coda I
C
Am
Am/G
D
F
- lone.
8vb
Am
Am/G
D
F
Am
Am/G

D.%% al Coda II
D
G
G/F
C/E
G7/D
137
Coda II
C
F/C
C
G/B
143
And the pia-no, it sounds like a
cresc.
ff
F/A
C/G
F
C/E
D
G
149
car-ni-val and the mi-cro-phone smells like a beer, and they
8vb
C
G/B
F/A
C/G
F
F/G
155
sit at the bar and put bread in my jar and say, "Man, what are you do-in' here?"
8vb

161
C
Am
Am/G
D/F♯
F
Oh, la, la, la, di, di, da.
mf
8vb
167
Am
Am/G
D/F♯
D
G
G/F
C/E
G7/D
La, la, di, di, da, da, dum.
(8)
175
C
G/B
F/A
C/G
Sing us a song, you're the pia - no man,
f
8vb
179
F
C/E
D
G
C
G/B
sing us a song to - night. Well, we're all in the mood for a
(8)

F/A
C/G
Fadd9/A
G9sus4
C
185
mel - o - dy
and you've got us
feel - in' al - right.
8vb
190
C
G/B
F/A
mf
8vb
194
C/G
F
F/G
C
(8)
198
F/C
Cmaj7
F/C
C
Dm7/C
C
rit.
202
F/C
Cmaj7
F/C
C
Dm7/C
C

PROMISE ME

Words and Music by Beverley Craven

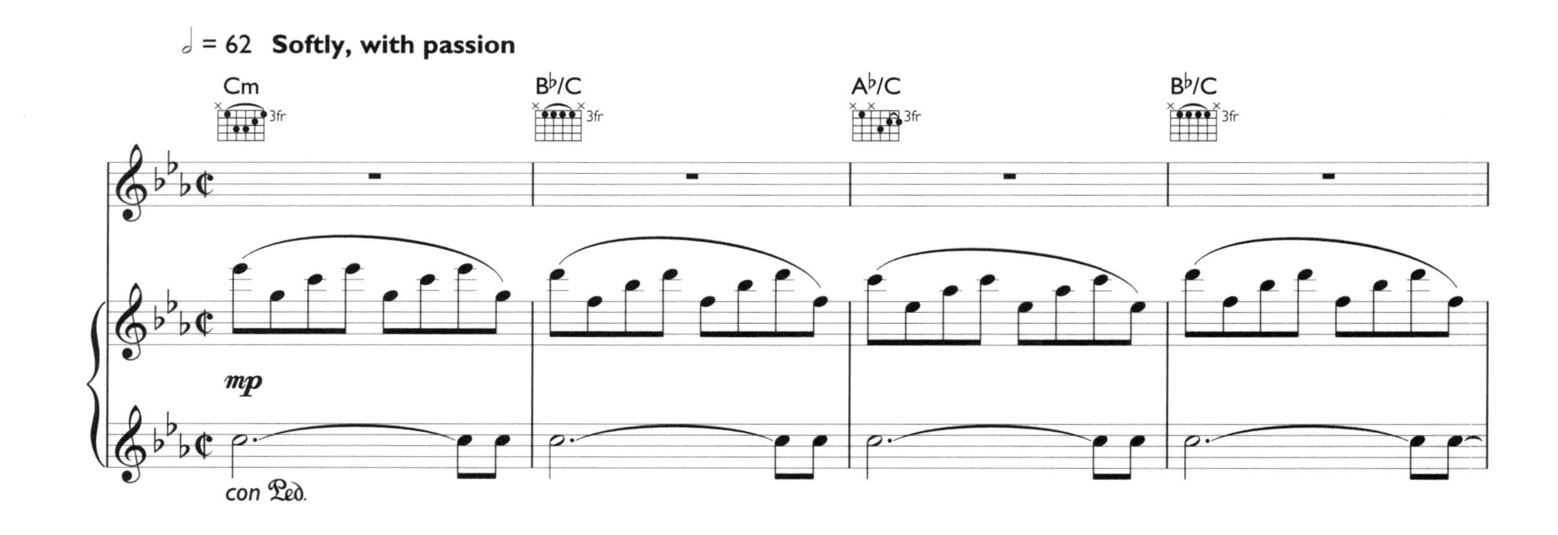

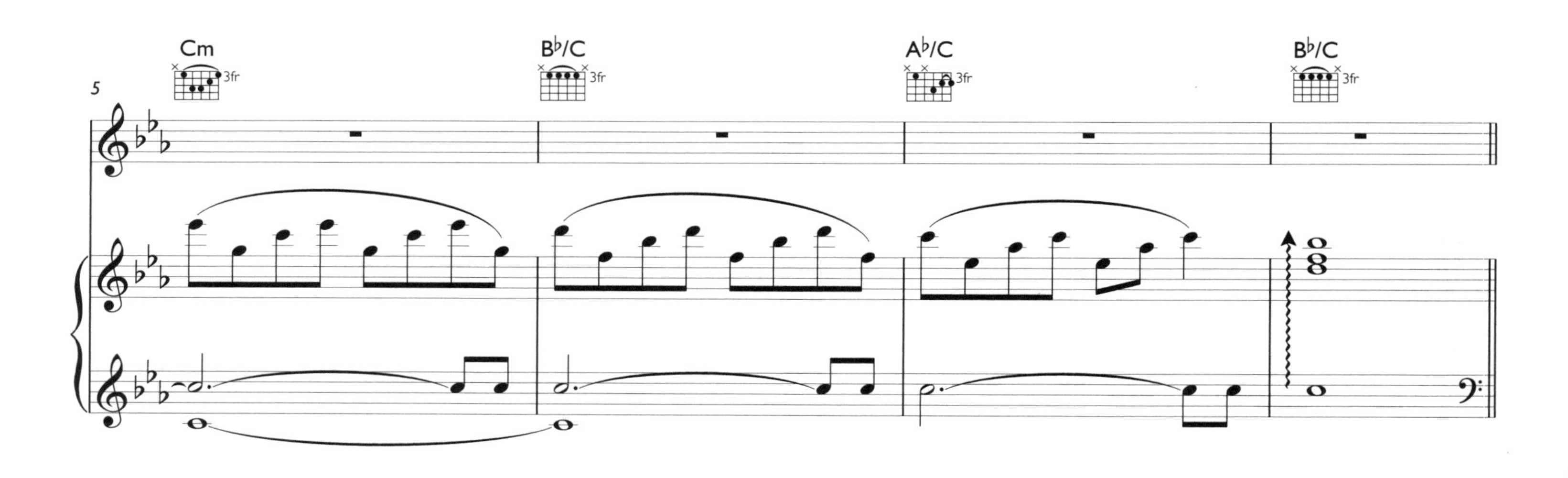

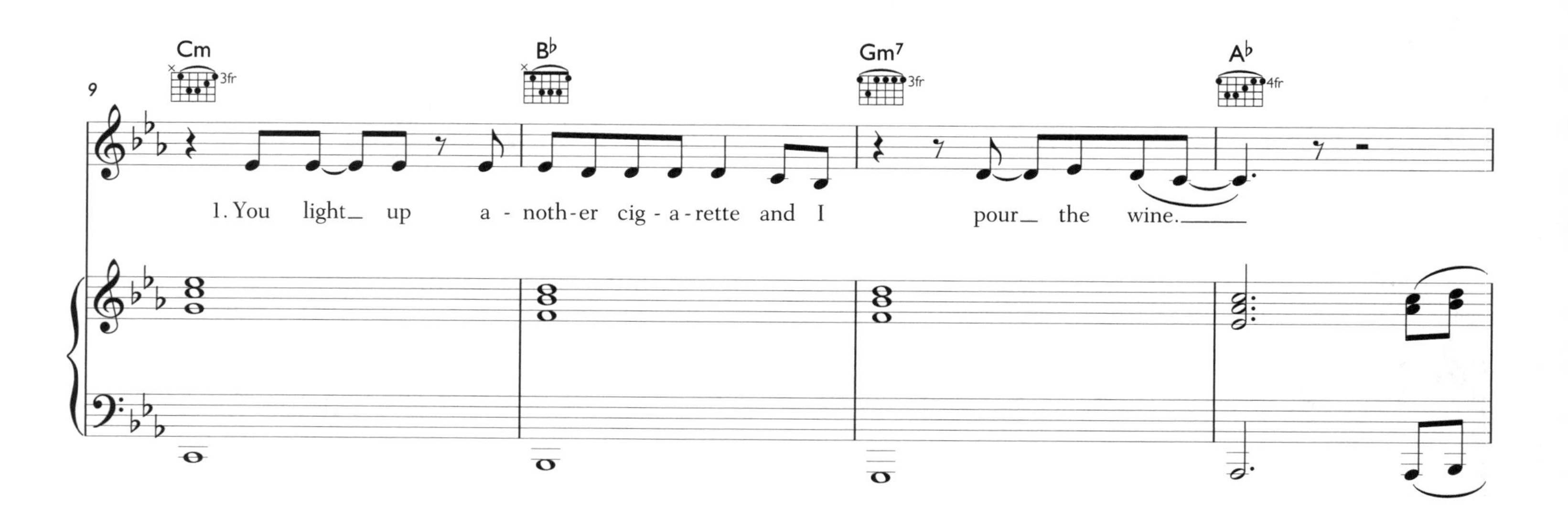

Cm
B♭
Gm7
A♭
It's four o' clock in the morn - ing and it's start - ing to get light.
Cm
B♭
E♭/G
A♭
Now I'm right where I wan - na be, lo - sing track of time, but I
Fm7
Gm
Cm
Cm/D
Cm/E♭
A♭
wish that it was still last night.
rit.
Gaug7
a tempo
Cm
B♭
2. You look like you're in a - noth - er world, but I

Gm7
A♭
Cm
B♭
29
can read your mind.
How can you be so far a-way,
sim.
Gm7
A♭
G/B
G
Cm
33
ly - ing by my side.
When I go a-way I'll miss you,
C/E
Fm
D♭
D♭/E♭
37
and I will be think - ing of you,
ev - 'ry night and day, just
A♭
Cm7
B♭m7
D♭/E♭
41
prom - ise me you'll wait for me, 'cause I'll be sa - ving all my love for you,

A♭
E♭/G
D♭add9/F
E♭/G
E♭7/G
and I will be home soon.
A♭
Cm7
B♭m7
Prom - ise me you'll wait for me, I need to know you feel
C
C/E
Fm(add9)
Fm
Dm7♭5
the same way too,
D♭
D♭/E♭
To Coda
A♭
Gaug7
and I'll be home, I'll be home soon.

Cm(add9)
B♭
Gm7
A♭
3fr
4fr
59
3
63
D.𝄋 al Coda
8
Coda
Cm7
B♭m7
67
Promise me you'll wait for me, 'cause I'll be saving all
D♭/E♭
E♭/G
70
my love for you, and I will be home soon.

D♭add9/F
E♭/G
E♭7/G
A♭
4fr
73
3
Prom - ise me you'll
Cm7
3fr
B♭m7
C
C/E
76
wait for me, I need to know you feel the same way
Fm(add9)
4fr
Fm
Dm7♭5
D♭
79
too,
and I'll be home,
D♭/E♭
A♭
4fr
rit.
82
I'll be home soon.

RAINING IN BALTIMORE

Words and Music by Adam Duritz, David Bryson,
Matt Malley, Steve Bowman and Charlie Gillingham

F
Dm
B♭sus2
C
To Coda
13
where you should be, no - one's a - round.
in - ten - tion of liv - ing this way.
way, but what would you change if you could?
17
I need a phone call,
I need a phone call,
21
I need a rain - coat,
I need a plane ride,
25
I need a big love,
I need a sun - burn,

B♭sus2
1.
F
I need a phone call.
I need a rain - coat.
2. These train
2.
F
Gm
F/A
C
B♭
And I get no ans - wers.
B♭
B♭/A
B♭/G
C
B♭
And I don't get no change.
B♭
B♭/A
B♭/G
C
B♭
It's rain - ing in Bal - ti - more, ba -

F
B♭sus2
F
47
-by, but ev-'ry-thing else is the
C
50
D.𝄋 al Coda
same.
3. There's things
𝄌 Coda
54 N.C.
B♭
F
I need a phone call,
may-be I should buy a
B♭
F
B♭
59
new car.
I can al-ways hear a freight train

F
B♭
64
baby if I listen real hard.
69
And I wish it was a small world.
Because I'm lonely
74
for the big towns,
I'd like to hear a little
79
guitar,
I guess it's time to put the top down.

F Bb F
85
I need a phone call.
Bb F Bb
90
I need a rain - coat,
I real - ly need a rain - coat...
F Bb F
96
I real - ly, real - ly need a rain - coat...
I real - ly,
Bb F Bb
102
real - ly, real - ly need a rain - coat...
I real - ly need a rain - coat...

ROCKET MAN

Words by Bernie Taupin
Music by Elton John

Gm7
3fr
Gm7/C
F/C
9
I miss the earth so much, I miss my wife;
Gm7
3fr
Gm7/C
Gm7/D
11
3
it's lone - ly out in space,
E♭
B♭add9/D
B♭/D
Cm
3fr
Cm11/B♭
13
on such a time - - - - - less flight
F/A
F/C
F7
E♭/F
15

B♭
B♭/D
E♭add9
And I think it's gon-na be a long, long time till touch down brings me round a-gain to find
I'm not the man they think I am at home, oh no, no, no: I'm a
C
Csus4
rock-et man.
Rock-et man burn-ing out his fuse up here
B♭sus4
B♭add9
a-lone.

Gm7
C9
Gm7
2. Mars ain't the kind of place to raise your kids; in fact, it's cold as hell,
mp
C7
B♭add9/D
E♭
B♭add9/D
B♭/D
Cm
Cm/B♭
and there's no one there to raise them if you did.
F/A
F/C
F
Gm7
C11
And all this sci - ence, I don't un - der - stand;
mf

Gm7
C9
Gm7/C
B♭/D
E♭
B♭/D
it's just my job five days a week: a rock-et man,
Cm
Cm7/B♭
F/A
F/C
F
E♭/F
a rock-et man.
B♭
B♭/D
E♭add9
And I think it's gon-na be a long, long time till touch down brings me round a-gain to find
B♭
B♭/D
E♭add9
B♭/D
I'm not the man they think I am at home, oh no, no, no: I'm a

45
C
Csus4
C/D
E♭add9
3fr
5fr
rock-et man.
Rock-et man
burn - ing out his fuse up here
47
B♭
B♭sus4
E♭
1.
a - lone.
2.
49
mp
B♭add9
6fr
And I think it's gon - na be a long, long time...
51
And I think it's gon - na be a long, long time...

E♭add9
5fr
B♭
B♭sus4
B♭add9
6fr
53
And I think it's gon - na be a long, long time...

E♭add9
5fr
B♭
B♭sus4
B♭add9
6fr
55
And I think it's gon - na be a long, long time...

E♭add9
5fr
B♭
B♭sus4
B♭add9
6fr
57
repeat to fade
And I think it's gon - na be a long, long time...

SMELLS LIKE TEEN SPIRIT

Words and Music by Kurt Cobain, Chris Novoselic and David Grohl

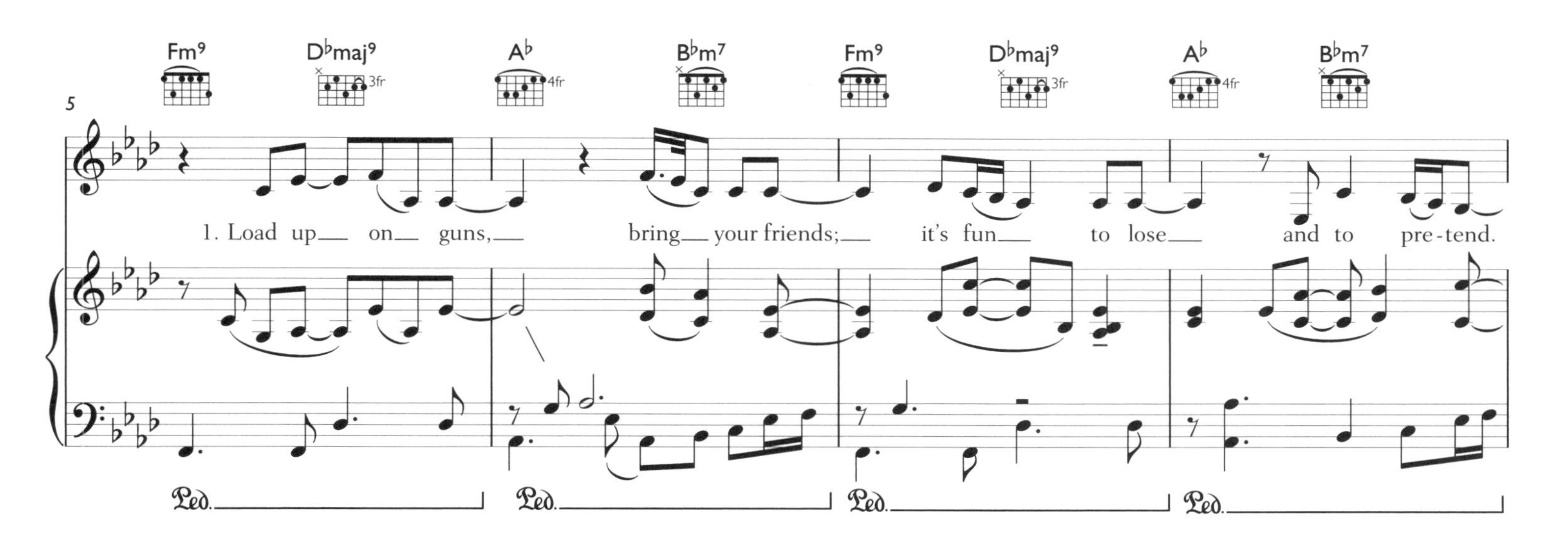

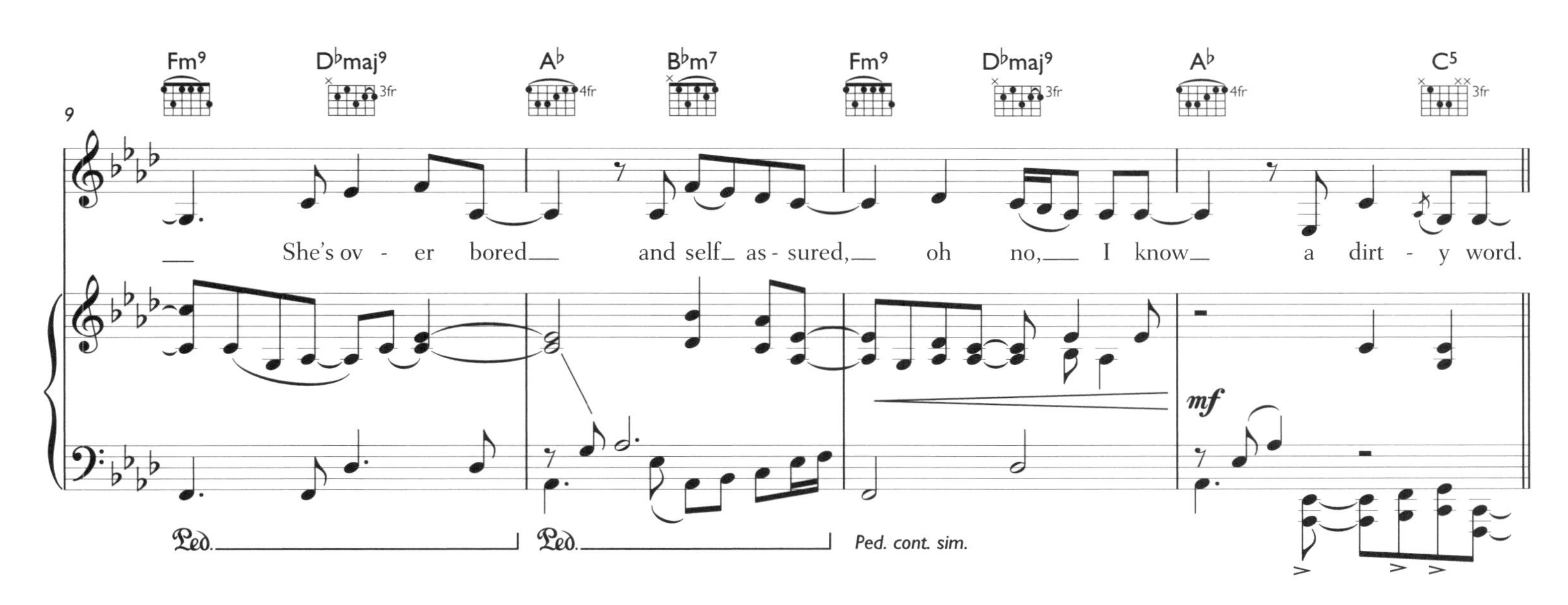

13
Fm9 D♭maj9 A♭maj7 B♭m7 Fm9 D♭maj7 A♭ Cm/B♭
Hel - lo, hel - lo, hel - lo, how low? Hel - lo, hel - lo. Ah.
mp
17
Fm9 B♭m A♭ D♭ Cm Fm9 B♭m Fm/C B♭m Cm
21
Fm9 D♭maj7 A♭ B♭m Fm9 D♭maj9 A♭add9 B♭m7 Cm7
2. I'm worse at what I do best, and for this gift I feel blessed.
25
Fm9 D♭maj9 A♭ B♭m Fm/C Fm9 D♭maj9 A♭ B♭m7 Cm
Our lit - tle group has al - ways been and al - ways will be, un - til the end.

Fm9 D♭maj7 A♭maj7 B♭m9 Fm9 D♭maj7 A♭maj7 B♭m6
29
Hel-lo, hel-lo, hel-lo, how low? Hel-lo, hel-lo. With the lights
Fm9 D♭(add♯4) A♭ B♭m7 Fm9 D♭(add♯4) A♭ B♭m7
33
out it's less dan-ger-ous. Here we are now, en-ter-tain us. I feel stu-
p
mp
cresc.
Fm9 D♭ A♭ B♭m7 Fm D♭ A♭ B♭m7
37
pid and con-ta-gious. Here we are now, en-ter-tain us, yes.
Fm9 D♭maj7 A♭add9 B♭m Fm/C Fm9 D♭ A♭ B♭m7 E♭
41
cresc.

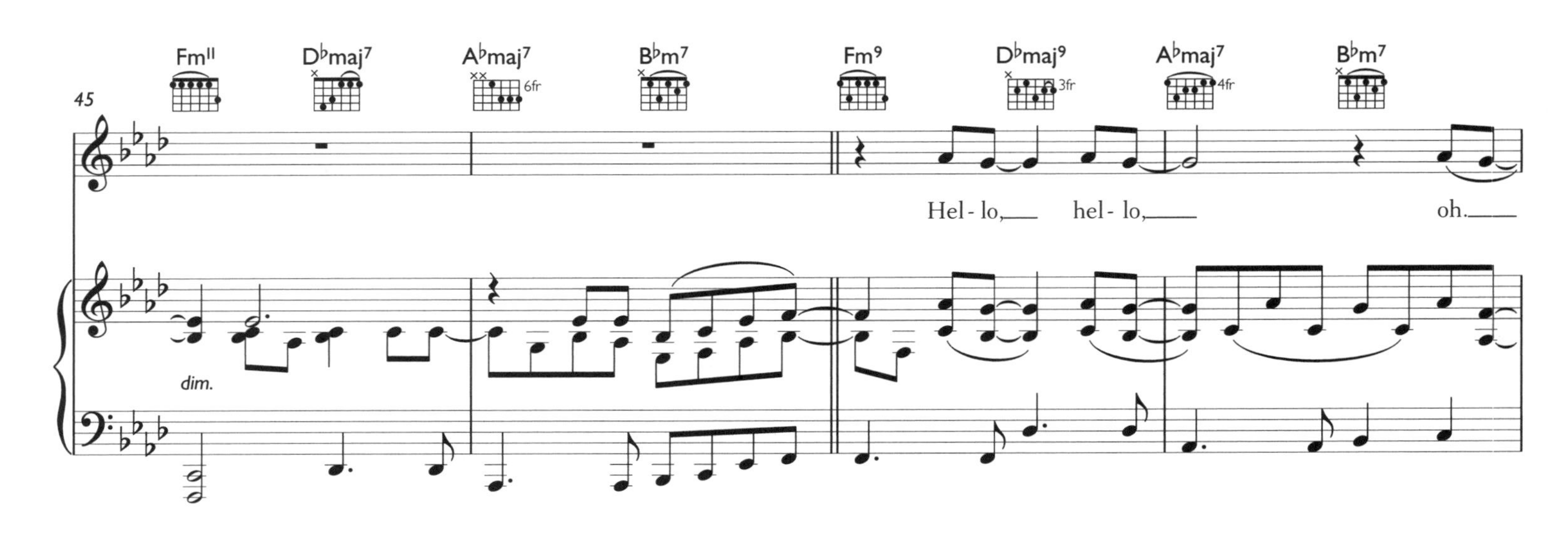
Fm11
D♭maj7
A♭maj7
6fr
B♭m7
Fm9
D♭maj9
3fr
A♭maj7
4fr
B♭m7
45
Hel - lo,
hel - lo,
oh.
dim.

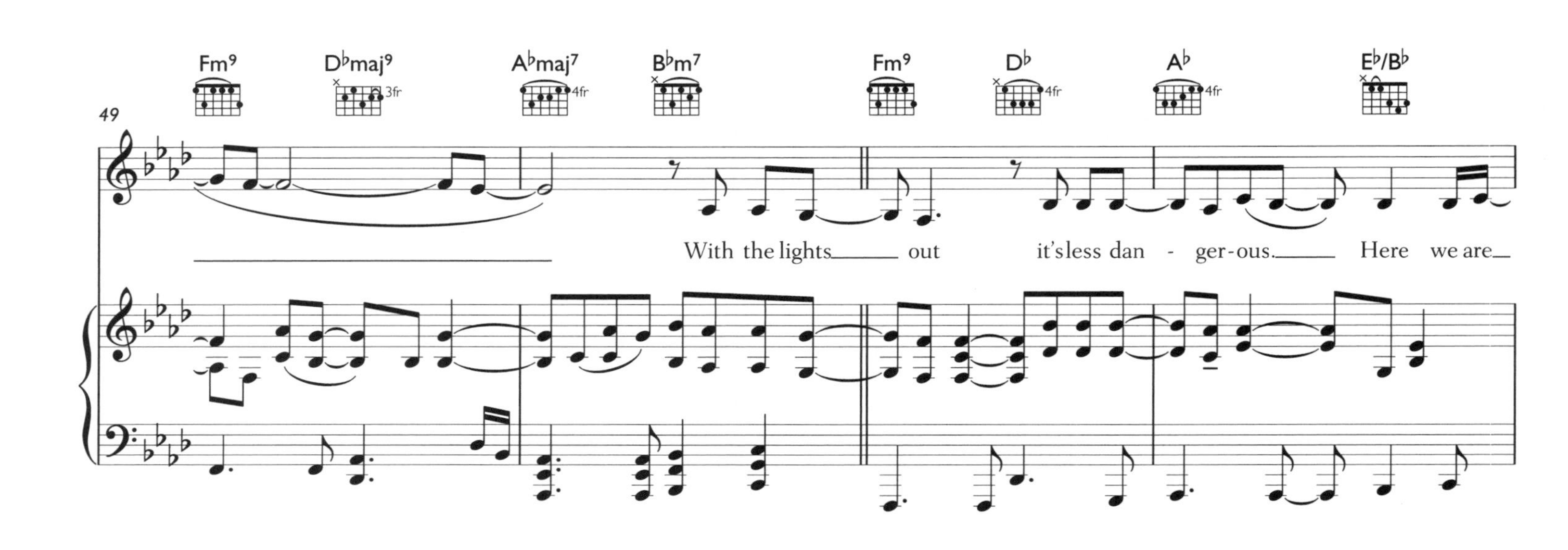
Fm9
D♭maj9
3fr
A♭maj7
4fr
B♭m7
Fm9
D♭
4fr
A♭
4fr
E♭/B♭
49
With the lights
out
it's less dan - ger - ous.
Here we are

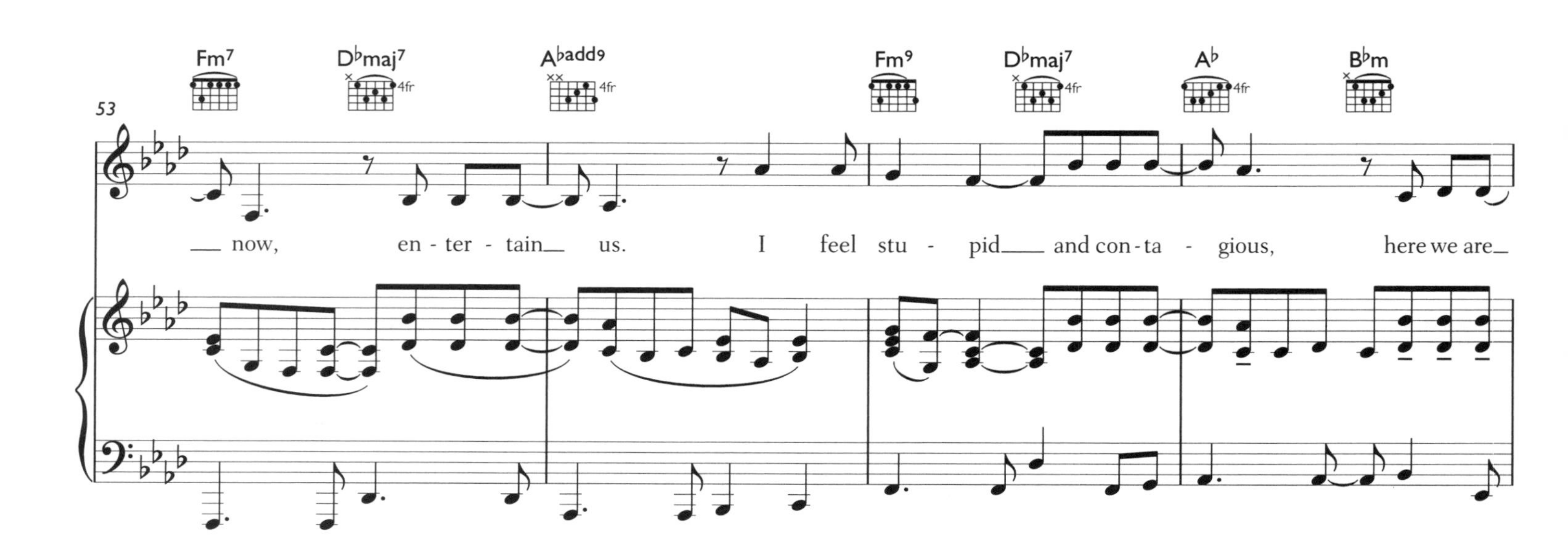
Fm7
D♭maj7
4fr
A♭add9
4fr
Fm9
D♭maj7
4fr
A♭
4fr
B♭m
53
now,
en - ter - tain
us.
I
feel
stu - pid
and con - ta - gious,
here we are

Fm9 D♭ A♭ B♭m Fm9 D♭(add♯4) A♭sus4 A♭ E♭7
9fr 4fr 4fr 4fr
57
now, en-ter-tain us. Yes, a mul-at - to, an al-bi - no, a mos-qui-
Fm D♭ A♭sus4 A♭ B♭m7 C5 Fm9 D♭maj7 A♭add9 B♭m7 Cm7
4fr 4fr 3fr 4fr 4fr 3fr
61
- to, my li-bi - do. A den-i - al, a den-i - al, a den-i-

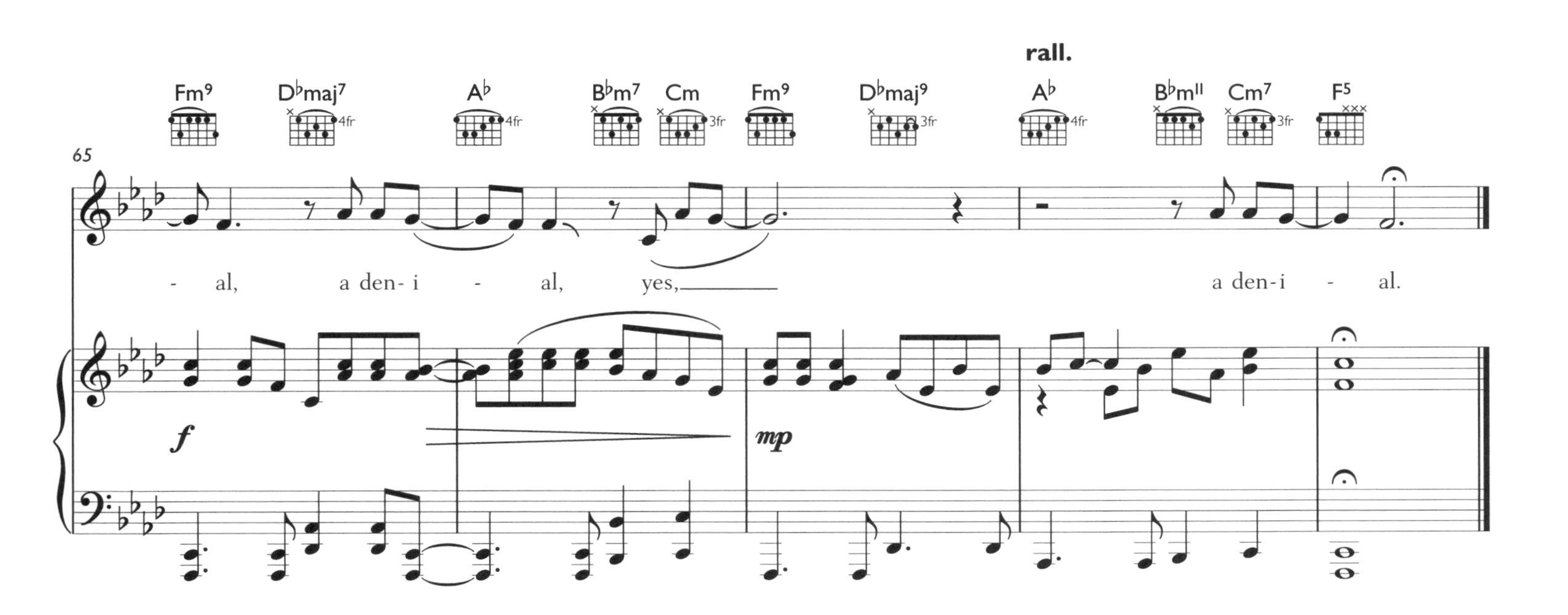
rall.
Fm9 D♭maj7 A♭ B♭m7 Cm Fm9 D♭maj9 A♭ B♭m11 Cm7 F5
4fr 4fr 3fr 3fr 4fr 3fr
65
- al, a den-i - al, yes, a den-i - al.
f
mp

SOMEBODY TO LOVE

Words and Music by Freddie Mercury

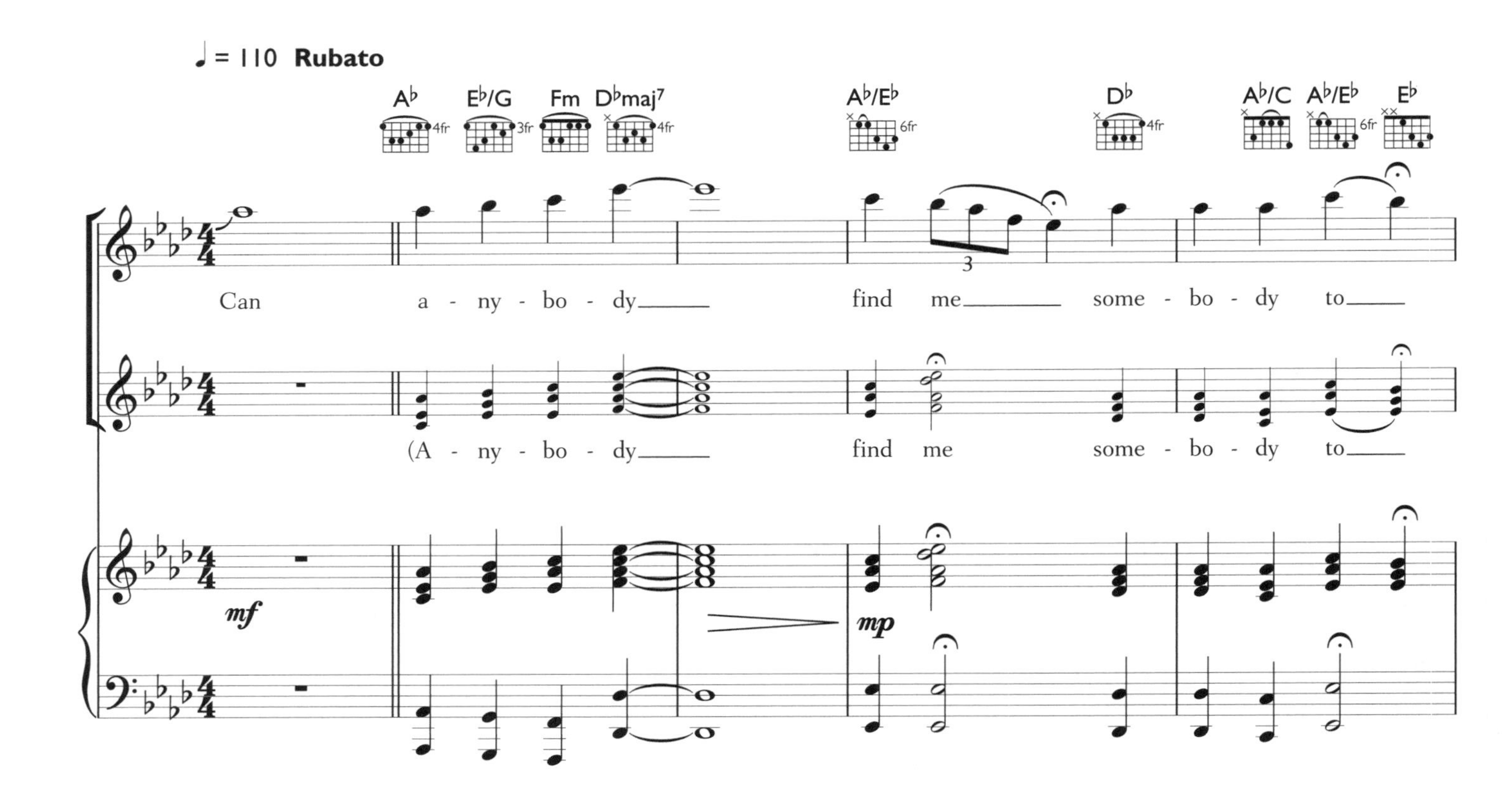

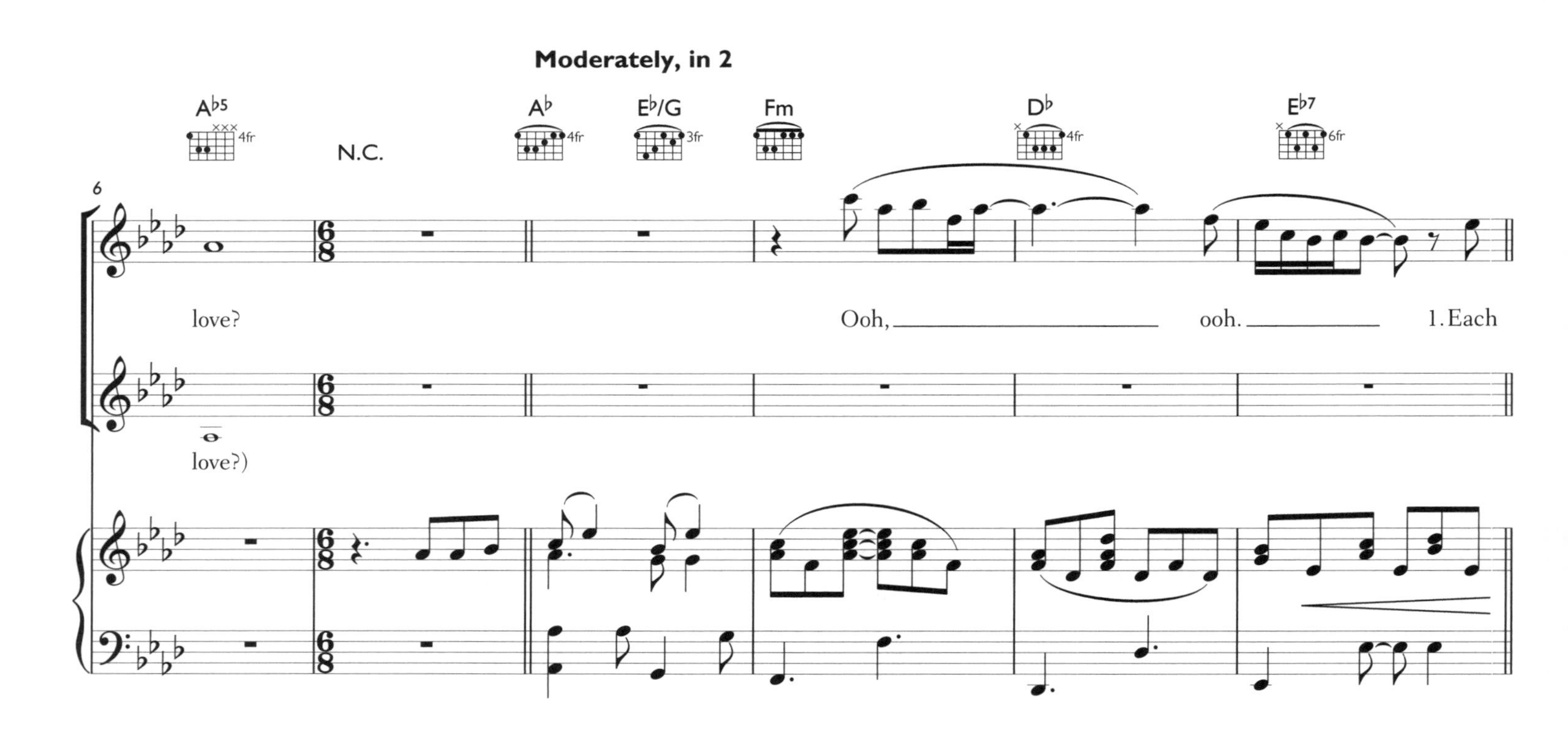

A♭ E♭/G Fm7 A♭ B♭ E♭
4fr 3fr 4fr 6fr 6fr
12
morn - ing I get up, I die a lit - tle; can bare - ly stand on my feet. Take a
(Take a look at your -
A♭ E♭/G Fm B♭ E♭
4fr 3fr 6fr 6fr
16
look in the mir - ror and cry, Lord, what you're do - ing to me. I have
3
- self in the mir - ror and cry yeah.)
A♭ B♭7 E♭ B♭7 E♭ D♭
4fr 6fr 6fr 6fr 6fr 4fr
20
spent all my years in be - liev - ing you, but I just can't get no re - lief, Lord,
(Ooh, be - liev - ing you, I just can't get no re - lief, Lord,

A♭
E♭/G
Fm7
D♭maj9
E♭11
24
some-bo-dy, ooh, some-bo-dy. Can a-ny-bo-dy find me some-bod-y to love?
some-bo-dy, some-bo-dy, a-ny-bo-dy find me.)
mp
f
A♭
A♭/G
Fm
D♭
E♭
29
yeah. 2. I work
mp
Ped.
Ped.
Ped.
A♭
E♭/G
Fm7
A♭
B♭
E♭
34
hard ev-'ry day of my life, I work 'til I ache my bones. At the
(He works hard.)
mf

A♭
E♭/G
Fm
B♭
38
end I take home my hard-earned pay all
(At the end of the day, goes home,
E♭
B♭7
E♭
41
on my own. I go down on my knees and I start to pray 'til the
goes home on his own. Down, knees, praise the Lord.
B♭7
E♭
D♭
A♭
44
tears run down from my eyes, Lord, some-bo-dy, ooh, some-bo-dy. Can
Ooh, Lord, some-bo-dy, please,
mp

E♭/G
Fm7
D♭maj9
E♭11
A♭
48
a - ny- bo - dy find me some - bo -dy to love?
a - ny- bo - dy find me.)
f
A♭9
D♭
D♭7
53
Ev - 'ry day, I've tried and I've tried and I've
(He works hard ev -'ry day, tried I've tried I've
f
G♭
58
tried, but ev - 'ry - bod - y wants to put me down, they say
tried. Ooh,

G♭m
B♭
I'm go - ing cra - zy.
They say I got a lot of wa - ter in my
ooh,
ah.
brain, but I got no com - mon sense, I got no - bo - dy left to be - lieve.
E♭II
He's got no - bo - dy left to be - lieve.
A♭
Cm/G
Fm7
B♭
Guitar solo
Yeah, yeah, yeah, yeah.)

82

A♭ E♭/G Fm7 D♭maj9 E♭11

Ooh, some - bo - dy, ooh, a - ny - bo - dy find me some -

some - bo - dy, some - bo - dy, a - ny - bo - dy find me,

mf *f*

A♭
A♭/G
Fm
D♭
E♭II
- bo-dy to love?
3. Got no
can a-ny-bo-dy find me some-one to
A♭
A♭/G
Fm7
A♭
B♭
E♭
feel, I got no rhy-thm, I'll just keep lo-sing my beat. I'm
love?)
(He'll just keep lo-sing and
A♭
E♭/G
Fm
B♭
E♭
O-K. I'm al-right, I ain't gon-na face no de-feat. I just
lo-sing. He's al-right, he's al-right, yeah.)

A♭
B♭
E♭
B♭
E♭
D♭
4fr
6fr
6fr
6fr
6fr
4fr
100
got-ta get out of this pris-on cell, some - day I'm gon-na be free, Lord.
(Ooh, this pris-on cell, some - day I'm gon-na be free, Lord.)

105
N.C.
(Find me some-bo-dy to love, find me some-bo-dy to love. Find me some-
pp
mp

110
-bo-dy to love, find me some-bo-dy to love. Find me some-bo-dy to love,

A♭
4fr
115
find me some - bo - dy to love. Find me some - bo - dy to love.
119
Find me some - bo - dy to love. Find me some -
122
- bo - dy to love, find me some - bo - dy to love.
126
Some - bo - dy, some - bo - dy, some - bo - dy, some - bo - dy, some - bo - dy, find me some - bo - dy, find me some -

A♭
E♭/G
Fm7
D♭maj9
E♭11
130
Can a - ny - bo - dy find me
- bo - dy to love. A - ny - bo - dy find me.)
ff
Free time
134
N.C.
some - bo - dy to love?
A♭
A♭/G
Fm
D♭
E♭
Free time
A♭
140
Repeat x6
ad lib. vocals
love.) (Find me some - bo - dy to love.
145
Find me, find me, find me, find me...

THIS HOUSE

Words and Music by Alison Moyet

B7/D#
Em
C
Am7
Bsus4
2fr
19
that used to be full of life, now it's home for no-one and his wife.
B
Em
G/D
C
24
It's a ho-vel and: (Who,) who can take your place?
Bsus4
2fr
B
Em
29
I can't face an - o - ther day, and (who,)
G/D
C
Bsus4
2fr
B
Esus4
34
who will shel- ter me? It's cold in here, co-ver me.

♩. = 52
Em
C
Em/B
A♯dim
B7sus4
B7
Em
C6
B7/D♯
Em
Em/D
3fr
2. Un - der these fin - ger - tips, a strange bo - dy rolls and dips I
C
Bsus4
2fr
B
Em
close my eyes and you're here a - gain. La - ter as
C6
B7/D♯
Em
C
day des - cends I'll shout from my win - dow to an - y - one list - 'ning

♩. = 𝅗𝅥
B
Em
62
I'm los - ing.
(Who,)
G/D
C
Bsus4
2fr
B
66
who can take your place?
I can't face an -
Em
G/D
C
71
- o - ther day.
And (who,)
who will shel - ter me?
Bsus4
2fr
B
Esus4
Em
76
It's cold in here,
co - ver me.

C
Cmaj7
Em
81
Oh, in a plague of hate - ful ques - tion - ing,
tap danc - ing ev - 'ry syl - la - ble from
E♭/B♭
E♭
84
ear to ear.
I hear the din of lov - ers joust - ing
when I'm hid - ing with my head to the
Em
G/D
C
88
wall.
So (who)
who will shel - ter me?
Bsus4
2fr
B
Esus4
Em
92
It's cold in here...

THE THINGS WE DO FOR LOVE

Words and Music by Eric Stewart and Graham Gouldman

E♭
G♭
12
drift - ed out to sea,
you lay your bets and then you
F
E♭m
D♭
A♭9sus4
14
pay the price: the things we do for love.
(The things we do for
D♭
B♭m7
16
Com - mu - ni - ca - tion is the
love.)

G♭
D♭
Fm/C
prob - lem to the an - swer,
you've got her num - ber and your
(Ah,
E♭
G♭
hand is on the phone,
the wea-ther's turned and all the
ah.
Ah,
G♭/F
F
E♭m
D♭
A♭9sus4
D♭
N.C.
lines are down; the things we do for love.
Like walk-ing in the
Ah,
ah,
the things we do for love.)

D♭add9
9fr
rain and the snow when there's no-where to go, and you're
(Rain and the snow when there's no-where to go, and you're
E♭m G♭/D♭ E♭m/D♭ A♭7/C A♭7 Adim7 B♭m B♭m7/A♭
4fr
feel - in' like a part of you is dy - ing, and you're look-ing for the an - swer in her eyes;
feel - in' like a part of you is dy - ing, and you're look-ing for the an - swer in her eyes;
G♭maj7 Gm7♭5 A♭7 Adim B♭m7 F♯m
4fr
you think you're gon-na break up, then she says she wants to make up.
you think you're gon-na break up, then she says she wants to make up.)

Broadly
G/A
D/A
Ooh, you make me love you,
(Ah,
Em7/A
D/A
G/A
ooh, you've got a way,
ooh, you had me
ah.
D/A
Am11
To Coda
crawl - ing up the wall,
ah.

B♭m7
Oo,
oo.)
G♭
D♭
Fm/C
E♭
E♭7
Bom, bom, bom, bom, bom, bom, bom, bom, bom, bom, bom, bom,
Guitar Solo
G♭
G♭/F
F
E♭m
D♭
A♭7sus4
D♭
N.C.
D.𝄋 al Coda
bom, bom, bom, bom, bom, bah, bom. Like walk-ing in the

Coda
Steadily, upbeat
B♭m7
G♭
3. A com-prom-ise would sure-ly help the sit-u-a - tion;
(Ah,
D♭
Fm/C
E♭
G♭
a - gree to dis-a - gree, but dis-a - gree to part.
When af - ter all it's just a
ah.
Ah,
G♭/F
F
E♭m
E♭m7
D♭
A♭9sus4
com-prom - ise of the things we do for love,
ah, ah, the things we do for

D♭
A♭7sus4
the things we do for love,
the things we do for
love,
the things we do for love,
ah,
love,
the things we do for
love.
The things we do for love, ah,
ah,
repeat to fade
love,
the things we do for
love.
The things we do for love, ah,
ah,)

THE WAY IT IS

Words and Music by Bruce Hornsby

17
Am7 Em7 D Cadd9 G D Cadd9
21
Am7 Em7 D Cadd9
1. Stand - ing in line marking time, wait - ing for the wel - fare dime,
2. "Hey, lit - tle boy, you can't go where the oth - ers go
(3.) passed a law in 'six - ty four to give those who ain't got a lit - tle more,
23
G D Cadd9
3
'cause they can't buy a job. The
'cause you don't look like they do." Said,
but it on - ly goes so far. 'Cause the
25
Am7 Em7 D Cadd9
man in the silk suit hur - ries by, as he catch - es the poor old la - dies' eyes,
"Hey, old man, how can you stand to think that way, did you
law don't change a - no - ther's mind when all it sees at the hir - ing time

G
D
Cadd9
Gadd9
Fmaj7
C
27
just for fun he says, "Get a job."
real-ly think a-bout it be-fore you made the rules?" He said, "Son...
is the line on the co-lour bar.
30
That's just the way it is,
some things will ne-ver change.
33
To Coda
That's just the way it is,
36
Am7
Em7
ah, but don't you be-lieve them.

1.
2.
G
D
Cadd9
Cadd9
Am
Em
39
2. They say
Ooh, yeah.
D
C
G
D
C
Am
Em
43
D
C
G
D
C
Am
Em
47
D
C
G
D
C
51
Am
Em
D
C
54

56
G
D
C
Am7
Em7
D
C
60
G
D
C
Gadd9
Fmaj7
C
63
Gadd9
Fmaj7
C
D.𝄋 al Coda
That's_ just the way it is,__
that's_ just the way it is._ 3. Well they
Coda
66
Gadd9
Fmaj7
C
Am7
Em7
that's_ just the way it is,__ it is,__ it is,__ it is.__
69
D
C
G
D
C

Am7
Em7
D
C
72
G
D
C
Am7
Em7
74
D
C
G
D
C
77
Am7
Em7
D
Cadd9
G
D
Cadd9
80
Gadd9
Fmaj7
C
Gadd9
Fmaj7
C
84

87
Gadd9
Fmaj7
C
90
Gadd9
Fmaj7
C
Gadd9
Fmaj7
C
93
Gadd9
Fmaj7
C
96
Gadd9
Fmaj7
C
Gadd9
Fmaj7
C
99
Gadd9
Fmaj7
C
repeat ad lib. to fade

WITHOUT YOU

Words and Music by Pete Ham and Tom Evans

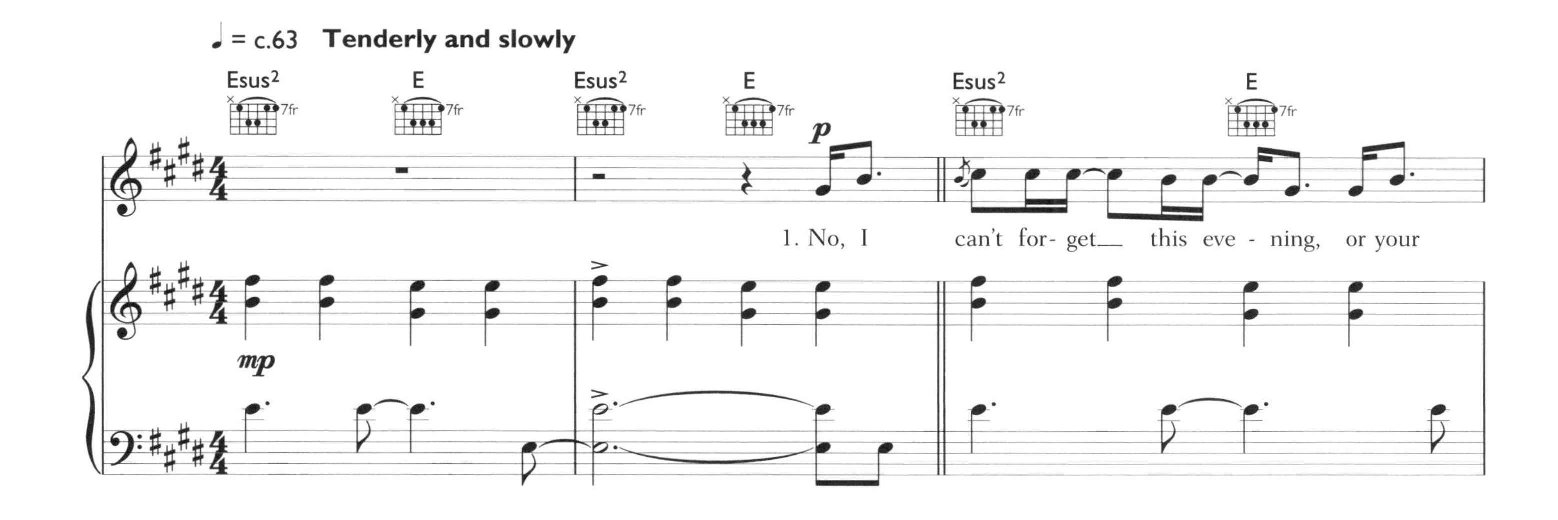

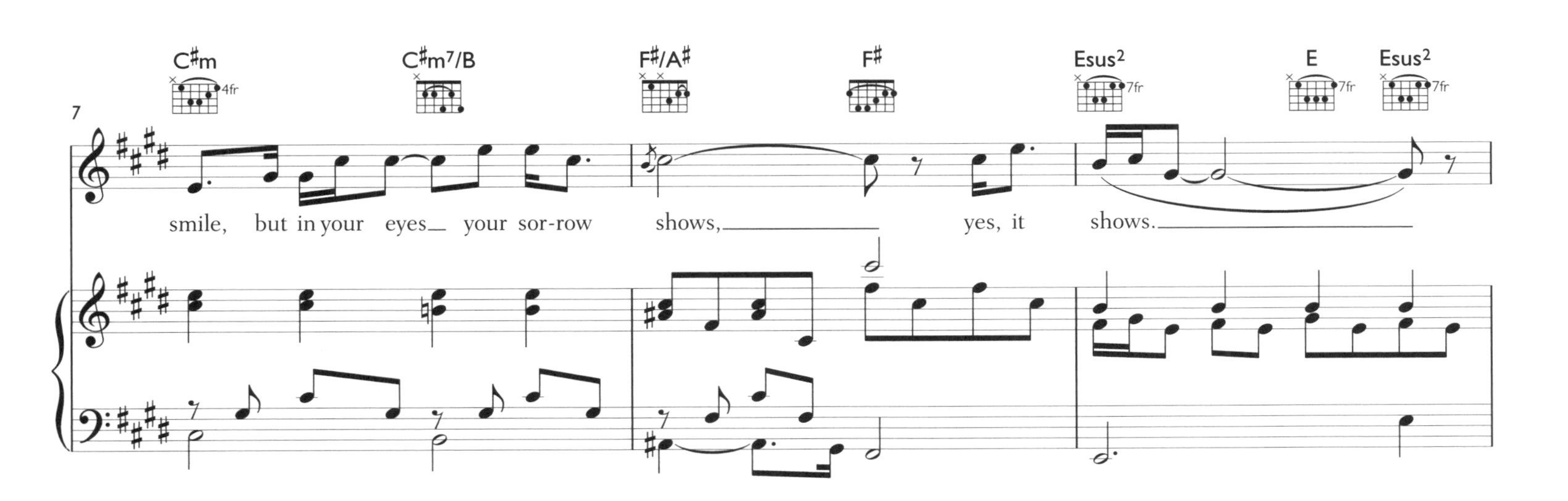

A/B
B7
Esus2
E
G♯m(add9)
G♯m
2. No, I can't for-get to-mor-row when I think of all my sor-row, well I
F♯m(add9)
F♯m
G♯
G♯7
C♯m
C♯m/B
had you there but then I let you go.
And now it's on-ly fair that I should let you know
F♯/A♯
F♯
E/G♯
Eadd9/G♯
what you should know.
mf
I can't
With a strong beat
C♯m7
live if liv-ing is with-out you, I can't live, I can't

A/B
B7
A/B
B7
E
C♯m7
4fr
give an - y - more
I can't live
if liv-ing is with-out you,
I can't
F♯m(add9)
F♯m
A/B
B7
live,
I can't give an - y - more.
3. Well, I
Softly
Esus2
7fr
E
7fr
G♯m(add9)
4fr
G♯m
4fr
can't for - get this eve - ning, or your
face as you were leav - ing, but I
F♯m(add9)
F♯m
G♯7
4fr
guess that's just the way the stor - y goes.
You al - ways

C♯m
4fr
C♯m/B
F♯/A♯
F♯add9
32
smile, but in your eyes your sor - row shows, yes, it

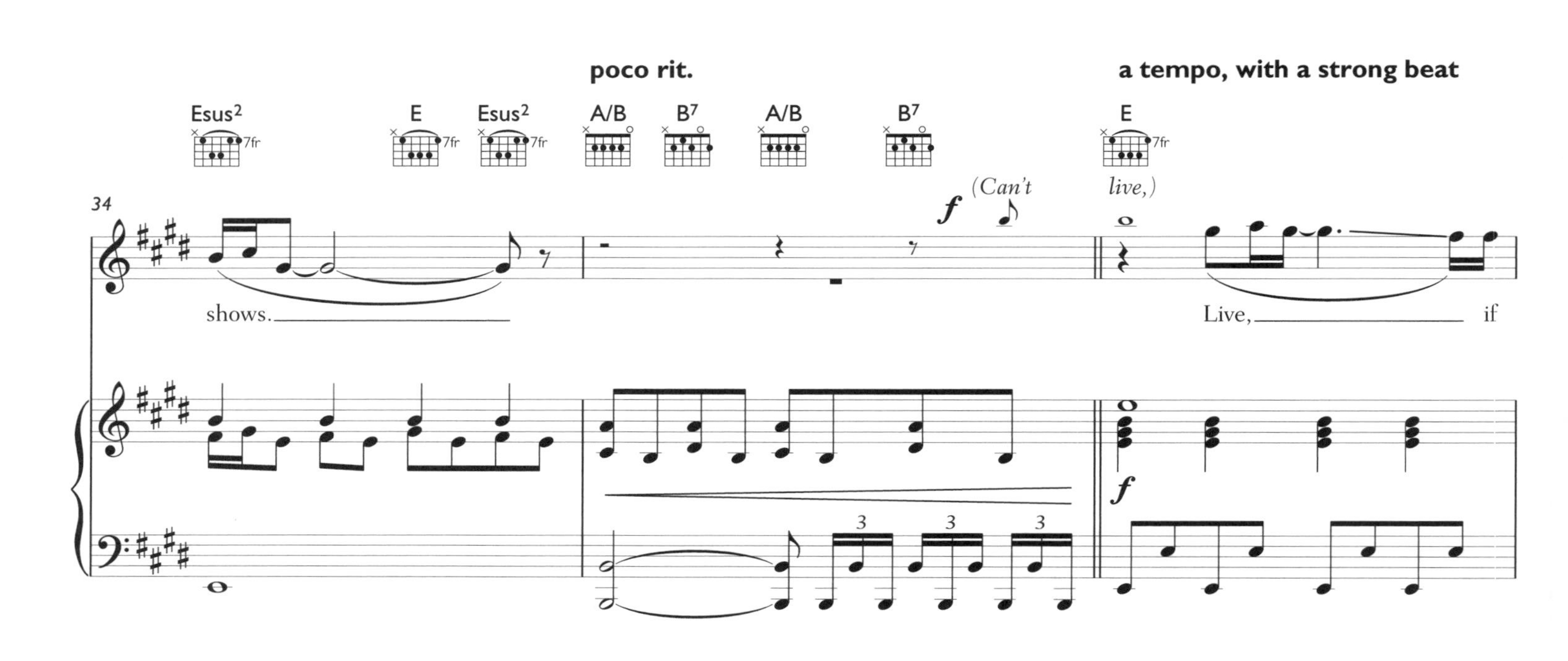
poco rit.
a tempo, with a strong beat
Esus2
7fr
E
Esus2
A/B
B7
A/B
B7
E
34
(Can't live,)
shows.
Live, if

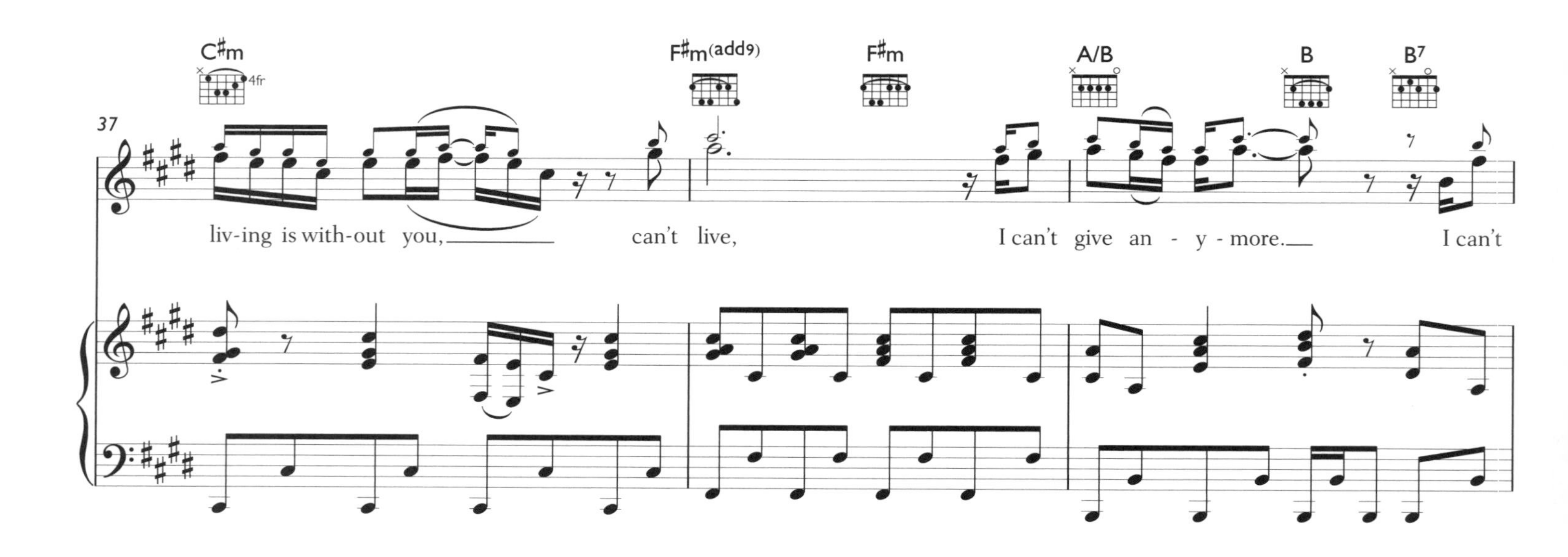
C♯m
4fr
F♯m(add9)
F♯m
A/B
B
B7
37
liv-ing is with-out you, can't live, I can't give an - y - more. I can't

E
C♯m
4fr
F♯m(add9)
F♯m
40
live if liv-ing is with-out you, I can't live, I can't
A/B
B7
E
C♯m
4fr
43
give an - y - more. Liv-ing is with-out you.
F♯m(add9)
F♯m
A/B
B7
Esus2
7fr
E
7fr
46
C♯m
4fr
F♯m(add9)
F♯m
A/B
B7
repeat to fade
49
3
3
3
3

WUTHERING HEIGHTS

Words and Music by Kate Bush

A
F
E
C♯
How could you leave me when I need-ed to pos-ess you, I hat-ed you, I
G♯
E♭m
G♭
Fsus4
loved you too.
Bad dreams in the night,
Too long I roam in the night,
mp
E♭m
G♭
Fsus4
E♭m
G♭
you told me I was go-ing to lose the fight.
Leave be-hind my
I'm com-ing back to his side to put it right.
Com-ing home to
Fsus4
Wuth-er-ing, Wuth-er-ing, Wuth-er-ing Heights
Wuth-er-ing, Wuth-er-ing, Wuth-er-ing Heights
Heath-

G♭ E♭m7 A♭ D♭ G♭
-cliff, it's me, your Cath-y, I've come home and I'm so cold,
A♭ D♭ G♭ G♭
let me in at your win-dow, oh Heath - oh.
1.3.
2.4.
To Coda
Amaj9 A F E
2. Ooh, it gets dark, it gets lone-ly on the oth-er side
mp
C♯ A F E
from you. I pine a lot, I find the lot falls through with-out

C♯
A
F
41
you.
I'm com-ing back, love,
cruel Heath-cliff,
E
C♯
G♯
D.𝄋 al Coda
44
my one dream,
my on-ly
mas-ter.
Coda
B♭m
A♭
G♭
E♭m7
D♭
47
Ooh, let me have it, let me grab your soul a-way. Ooh,
f
51
let me have it, let me grab your soul a-way.

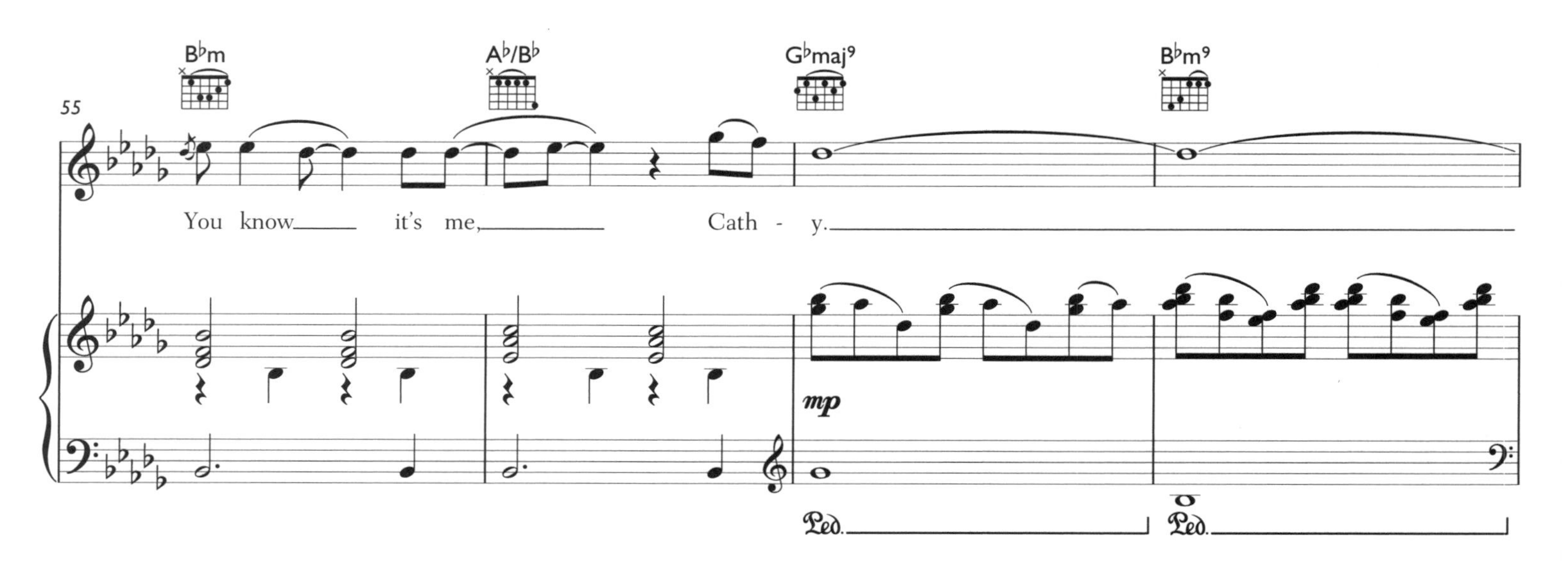
B♭m
A♭/B♭
G♭maj9
B♭m9
55
You know it's me, Cath - y.
mp
Ped.
Ped.

G♭
E♭m7
A♭
4fr
D♭
59
Heath - cliff, it's me, your Cath-y, I've come home and I'm
f
Ped.

G♭
A♭
4fr
D♭
G♭
63
repeat to fade
so cold, let me in at your win - dow, oh Heath -

ISBN10: 0-571-52540-7
EAN13: 978-0-571-52540-9

Faber Music Limited, Burnt Mill, Elizabeth Way, Harlow CM20 2HX England
Tel: +44 (0) 1279 82 89 82 Fax: +44 (0) 1279 82 89 83
sales@fabermusic.com fabermusic.com

A superb collection of songs from some of the greatest contemporary singer-songwriters. Transcribed for piano and voice, with guitar chord boxes.

ISBN10: 0-571-52581-4
EAN13: 978-0-571-52581-2

To buy Faber Music publications or to find out about the full range of titles available please contact your local retailer or Faber Music sales enquiries:

Faber Music Limited, Burnt Mill, Elizabeth Way, Harlow CM20 2HX England
Tel: +44 (0) 1279 82 89 82 Fax: +44 (0) 1279 82 89 83
sales@fabermusic.com fabermusic.com